ATLAS
of
LOST CIVILIZATIONS

Copyright © 2025 by Schiffer Publishing, Ltd.

Originally published as Atlas des peuples disparus by
Flammarion, Paris © 2022
Translated from the French by Rebecca DeWald.

Library of Congress Control Number: 2024946209

Edited by Ian Robertson
Designed by Karin Doering-Froger
Type set in Serenity/DTLParadox

ISBN: 978-0-7643-6951-3
Printed in China

Published by Schiffer Publishing, Ltd.
4880 Lower Valley Road
Atglen, PA 19310
Phone: (610) 593-1777; Fax: (610) 593-2002
Email: info@schifferbooks.com
Web: www.schifferbooks.com

For our complete selection of fine books on this and related
subjects, please visit our website at www.schifferbooks.com.
You may also write for a free catalog.

Schiffer Publishing's titles are available at special discounts
for bulk purchases for sales promotions or premiums. Special
editions, including personalized covers, corporate imprints,
and excerpts, can be created in large quantities for special
needs. For more information, contact the publisher.

DOMINIQUE LANNI

ILLUSTRATIONS BY CAMILLE RENVERSADE

ATLAS
of
LOST CIVILIZATIONS

SCHIFFER
PUBLISHING

4880 Lower Valley Road • Atglen, PA 19310

CONTENTS

For Mathilde,
Gone too soon, an angel among angels.
D.L.

SURVIVING OR DISAPPEARING

Oh Mexica, come running, your enemies have come out, they have emerged secretly!" Then another person shouted, on top of [the temple of] Huitzilopochtli; his crying spread everywhere, everyone heard it. He said, "Oh warriors, oh Mexica, your enemies are coming out, let everyone hasten with the war boats and on the roads!

—Anonymous, *The Florentine Codex*

In the Euphrates valley, an industrious, ingenious, and brilliant civilization developed and flourished as early as the fourth millennium BCE: the Sumerians. They invented what remains to this day one of the oldest forms of writing in the world, diversified the uses of the wheel, and founded the first cities. Then, they mysteriously vanished in what texts from the Third Dynasty describe as a phenomenal cataclysm.

Beyond the exceptional climatic upheaval it caused, the reaction of the Mayans to a terrible drought hitting a large part of the globe (the Tang dynasty in faraway China was also affected by it at the same time) led to the collapse of their city-states. Like a game of dominoes, the large-scale deforestation they caused depleted the soil. The lack of resources pitted city-states against each other, triggering wars and migrations. The Mayan civilization did not survive. Their Aztec neighbors also enjoyed a golden age, reigning from the start of the fourteenth century until the arrival of the Spanish conquistadors in what is now Mexico. They developed a sophisticated civilization, although they worshiped the sun in a particularly bloody man-

ner. The Aztecs were keen observers of the stars and invented a complex calendar that governed all the events of their lives. In a sad twist of fate, it was this very calendar that hastened their demise. The fifty-second year of the cycle was to mark the return of the god Quetzalcóatl. It coincided with the year 1519 of the Gregorian calendar and the arrival of bearded men riding horses and wearing helmets. To their great misfortune, the Aztecs mistook them for divine creatures, and their demise was as bloody as it was swift. Just three generations after the arrival of the conquistadors, Spanish chroniclers were already trying to salvage the last vestiges of this civilization and retrace its history.

Mass slaughter and genocide were not exclusive to ancient times, barbaric peoples, or expeditions in search of precious gold. In the nineteenth century, the English, considered one of the most civilized people in the world, decided to deport en masse their convicts and citizens they deemed undesirable to the end of the world—to Australia and Tasmania—and to drive the natives out like cattle. The Aboriginal Tasmanians revolted and confronted the English. But their numbers, their rudimentary weapons, and their lack of combat experience led to their downfall: they were decimated and herded into reserves, where the last of them died in the 1870s. The last survivor, named Truganini, died in 1876.

In the 1940s, on the edge of Tierra del Fuego, in a desolate, rocky landscape whipped by icy winds, the ethnologist José Emperaire watched helplessly as the last of the Alakaluf disappeared. Their fifty or so members, most of whom were suffering from congenital diseases and debility, died out one after the other, in most cases before reaching their forties.

In the late 1960s, American anthropologist Colin Turnbull warned the international community of the tragic extinction of the Ik people, an ethnic group of the Great Lakes region of Africa who had been displaced by the Ugandan government, which had created a nature park on their ancestral hunting grounds. Distraught by the fact they were reduced to depending on the state, they turned their backs on values such as mutual aid, solidarity, and altruism; became individualist; and turned to theft. They never recovered from this upheaval.

The Sumerian civilization, the Mayans, the Aztecs, the Aboriginal Tasmanians, the Alakaluf, and the Ik people vanished. So too did the peoples of the Indus Valley, the Nivkh people and the Selk'nam people. The Anasazi, whose villages carved in stone in the Mesa Verde mountains are extraordinary reminders of their presence in the world, disappeared just like the many Native American tribes who were defeated, massacred, and then corralled into reservations during the Gold Rush.

Paradoxically, tribes and peoples composed of thousands of individuals were not the only ones to die out: civilizations numbering millions of people that had prospered for centuries, founded political institutions and cities, devised ingenious irrigation systems, and developed science, technology, and the arts to the highest level, either died out or came to a spectacular halt. The Mali Empire, the Songhai Empire, and the Inca Empire all succumbed to this very fate, as did the inhabitants of the Pitcairn, Henderson, and Easter Islands at the same time.

Civilizations numbering millions of people that had prospered for centuries, founded political institutions and cities, devised ingenious irrigation systems, and developed science, technology, and the arts to the highest level, either died out or came to a spectacular halt.

Sadly, there is a long list of lost civilizations and peoples whose writings, artifacts, and ruins are all that remain to tell the story of who they were and, in some cases, the circumstances in which they died out. While the causes of the disappearance of many peoples and civilizations are well known, others have not revealed all their secrets and are still the subject of heated debate today.

Despite how events and upheavals unfolded, one certainty remains: these civilizations wanted to survive. They believed they could appease the wrath of the gods and triumph over their enemies and circumstances.

This is how they fell.

THE SUMERIANS

"Since Elam. Since Akkad. Since Sumer."

To this day, Sumer is considered the earliest known civilization and the one that invented writing, agriculture, and urban planning. The civilization emerged and prospered in the fourth millennium BCE in Mesopotamia, which was also known as the "land between two rivers" because it was located between the Euphrates River and the Tigris River. The Sumerians built and developed several cities that became hierarchical city-states governed by a priest king.

Around 3300 BCE, the city-state of Uruk began to flourish and soon outshone other city-states by its size, its population of several tens of thousands, and its beauty. It is also said that the legend of Gilgamesh originated in Uruk. Where did the Sumerians come from? The Persian Gulf? India? The farthest reaches of Asia? Or did they come from the sea, as some eloquent poems suggest?

Tombs and buildings were richly decorated and adorned with frescoes that praised rulers and divinities alike, testifying to the wealth of the owners as well as the artistic and comfortable way of life.

As the third millennium dawned, the two cities of Kish and Nippur were locked in an intense rivalry. To a lesser extent, the cities of Ur, Uruk, Lagash, Girsu, and Umma grew in a continuous state of conflict. Over the course of the millennium, the city of Ur blossomed. It became the civilization's most famous city, namely because Abraham was born there. It is also in this city that, for economic and administrative reasons, writing was first invented. The first cuneiform writings, examples of which have been excavated by the thousands, were engraved with the tip of a reed on clay tablets and painted on cylinder seals. Tombs and buildings were richly decorated and adorned with frescoes that praised rulers and divinities alike, testifying to the wealth of the owners, as well as the artistic and comfortable way of life.

To sow and irrigate their fields, the Sumerians invented and perfected tools such as the plow and seed drill, as well as an irrigation system, enabling them to obtain good harvests. Sumerians were ingenious farmers and remarkable shepherds able to capitalize on rearing tens of thousands of sheep. They were also engineers and built factories to develop the textile industry. Although they did not invent the wheel, they were the first to use it to get around by mounting it on vehicles. They were also brilliant mathematicians and exceptional astronomers: they invented the sexagesimal system, which consists of dividing time in units of 60, and provided precious knowledge of the stars to generations

that followed. Their neighbors, the Akkadians, were so enthralled by their modern ways and their wealth that they migrated en masse, eventually making up a sizable share of the workforce over the decades.

The priest kings were always eager to assert their power and extend their hegemony, launching their armies into destructive, ruinous, and endless wars.

Alongside these extraordinary developments, the civilization's city-states competed in more than just opulence, knowledge, and technical and cultural influence. The priest kings were always eager to assert their power and extend their hegemony, launching their armies into destructive, ruinous, and endless wars. But in 2340 BCE, an Akkadian named Sargon, descendant of the families that had migrated to Sumer early on and borrowed their customs, values, religion, and writings, was at the head of an impressive army. He united the Semitic factions, raised a gigantic army, and defeated the Sumerian city-states one by one. After consoli-

dating the position of king and giving it a divine character, he transferred the power to the city of Akkad, in the Akkadian Empire.

Akkadian rule was extremely short lived and lasted no more than a century. A long poem from the Third Dynasty and recorded on tablets found at Nippur attributed the fall of the Akkadian Empire to a curse. It claimed that the ruler, Naram-Sin, had offended the gods when he ordered the looting of the temple of Enlil, the main deity associated with the wind, air, earth, and storms. But it was in fact the revolts, civil wars, and incessant revolutions waged by the Sumerians that caused the downfall of the empire.

The rapid decline of the Akkadians facilitated the return to power of the Sumerians. Gudea, the "architect king," succeeded the last Akkadian ruler and inaugurated the Third Dynasty of Ur. He carried out far-reaching reforms as soon as he was enthroned, pulling the population out of its debts and misery and putting an end to popular unrest. The return of Sumerian rulers enabled city-states such as Ur, the new great capital, and its rival city Lagash to rise from their ashes and thrive, welcoming a population of up to 40,000 inhabitants. Gudea's successors contributed to the prosperity and greatness of the civilization.

However, the revival of the Sumerian cities would also prove to be short lived. At the turn of the second millennium, after a little less than a century and a half of peace, the people were once again tired of the extortions, iniquities, and broken promises of their rulers and turned against the king, the priests, and the elites. The unrest was followed by revolts that ended in chaos, the destruction of the city of Ur, and the downfall of the Third Sumerian Dynasty.

For a long time, invasions by warrior peoples such as the Amorites, Kassites, and Elamites; climatic disasters from droughts to floods and volcanic eruptions; and even meteorite falls (ancient texts mention a cataclysm and a sudden disappearance in a terrible crash) all were considered possible explanations for the destruction of Ur and the end of Sumer. By the year 2000 BCE, when the Amorites swept through the region, Ur had already fallen for several years.

"The Lament for Ur," or "Lamentation over the City of Ur," is a poem that tells of the fall of this powerful civilization, the first of this size in the history of humanity. Accompanied by visions of horror, it also delivers a warning full of wisdom for future generations:

"From time immemorial, when the Land was founded, until people multiplied, who has ever seen a reign last for ever? / The blood of the Lands, along with bronze and lead, pile up; / Its corpses, like fat left in the sun, melt away of themselves. / Its men, which no helmet can protect, struck down by an axe; / Like a gazelle caught in a trap, their mouths bite the dust . . . / Mothers and fathers who did not leave their houses were con-sumed by fire; / Children lying in their mothers' arms were carried off like fish by the waters. . . / May this disaster be entirely destroyed! / May the door be closed on it, like the great city-gate at night-time!"

In collective memory, the city-states of Ur, Lagash, Adab, and Kish gave way to a Mesopotamian city destined for an extraordinary fate: Babylon. It was in Babylon that the ziggurat of Etemenanki was built. With its temple of the foundations of Heaven and Earth on top of a tiered pyramid nearly 100 meters high, the ziggurat was dedicated to the cult of the god Marduk. It is associated with the biblical myth of the Tower of Babel, according to which men, filled with pride and arrogance, wanted to design a building that would let them reach God. In return, God punished them by multiplying languages to prevent them from understanding each other. But that is another story . . .

The unrest was followed by revolts that ended in chaos and the destruction of the city of Ur and the downfall of the Third Sumerian Dynasty.

THE HARAPPANS

In the Indus valley

During the seventh millennium BCE, several ethnic groups settled in the Indus valley. They began rearing cattle and sheep, cultivating cereals, and creating ceramic objects. From the sixth to the third millennia BCE, they learned to perfect their skills and techniques, creating finely worked pottery and small statues, and discovered how to forge copper. In the middle of the third millennium BCE, Harappa, Kalibangan, and Mohenjo-daro became large and prosperous fortified cities. These booming, homogeneous cities experienced such an expansion that archeologists referred to their populations as the peoples of the Indus civilization.

Six hundred years was the time that separated the rise of these peoples and their disappearance and subsequent assimilation by neighboring communities. How did these peoples, whose level of civilization was among the highest of the Bronze Age, disappear as suddenly as they appeared?

The Harappans built their towns and cities in verdant valleys on either side of the 2,000-mile-long Indus River. Over time, the largest of these cities grew to a population of 40,000. Their growth and prosperity derived from the abundant harvesting of cereals, cotton, and vegetables, as well as trade exchanges, facilitated by the river, with Lower Mesopotamia and Persia. Mohenjo-daro and Harappa, in present-day Pakistan, were built thanks to a system of weights and measures. Their size and configuration, which followed a grid pattern and geometrical distribution, made them particularly fascinating. Their designers were both ingenious architects and undoubtedly among the first great town planners in history. The houses that presumably belonged to the noble class had baths, wells, and toilets connected to an extended water drainage system. But while archeologists uncovered wealthy homes, there were no signs of palaces. How was this civilization organized? What authority did they obey? Was there a caste system? To this day, details of how the Harappans functioned remain an enigma. Likewise, only few weapons were unearthed, which could suggest that these peoples were peaceful, and their writing, which specialists are only just beginning to decipher, is also still a mystery. It was climate change that caused the undoing of this brilliant civilization. Harvests were no longer sufficient to feed the population, and trade dried up. The peoples of the Indus valley declined, tried to adapt, then migrated before merging with other cultures.

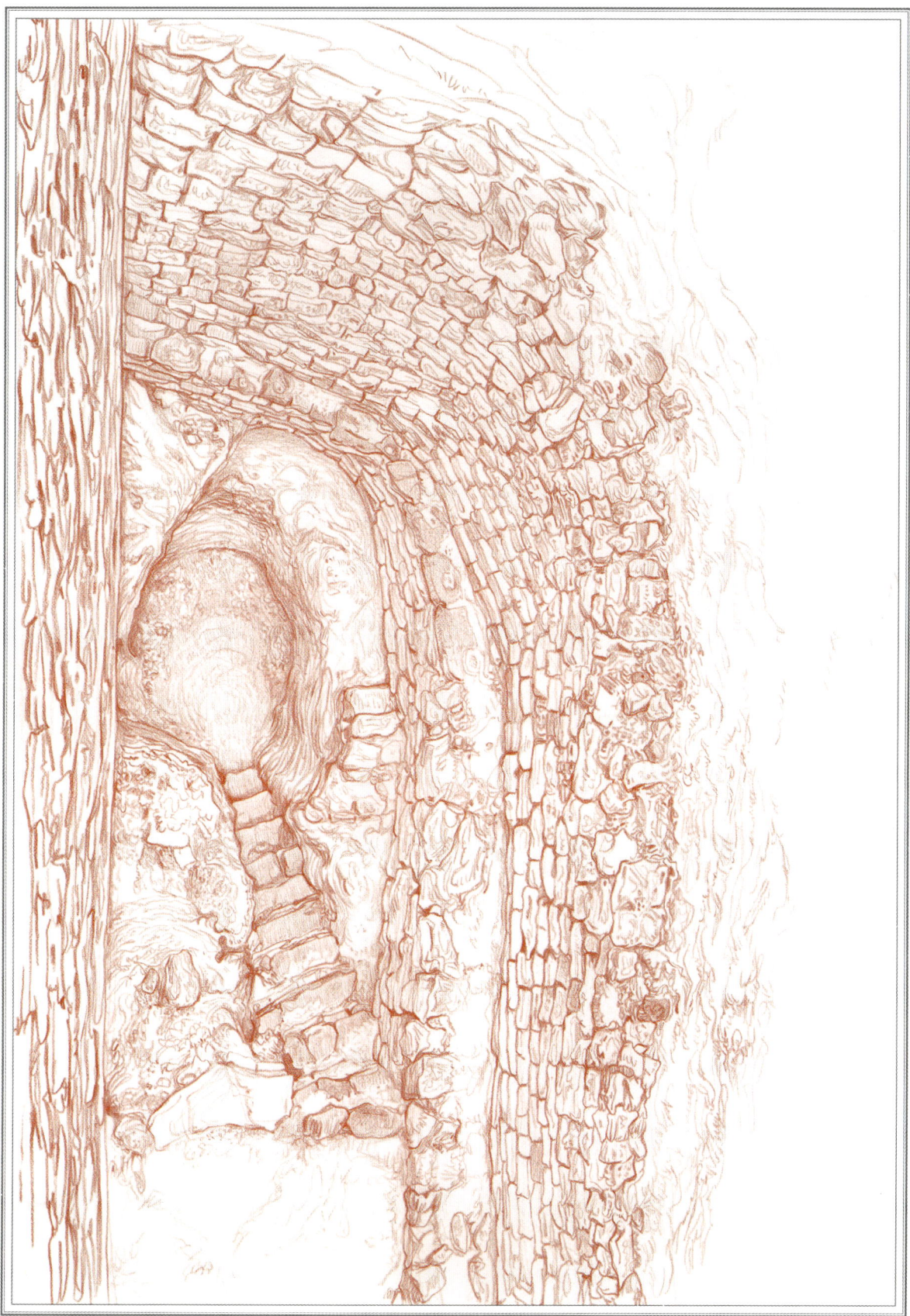

THE OLMECS

....

In the land of the jaguar sun

....

Despite its somewhat blurred affiliations, the distant Olmec civilization was probably the mother of pre-Columbian civilizations and Mesoamerican cultures. Who were the Olmecs, and where did they come from? It seems that some 2,500 years BCE, several ethnic groups speaking different languages came together. Over the centuries, other ethnic groups joined and together they formed a brilliant civilization that, at its height, ruled over an immense territory stretching from the Gulf of Mexico to present-day Costa Rica.

The mother of pre-Columbian civilizations and Mesoamerican cultures.

The Olmecs, whose original name, Olmeca, means "people of the land of rubber" in the Nahuatl language, spared no effort to tame a rather hostile environment. Ingenious scientists and skilled craftsmen developed and mastered techniques that enabled the civilization to achieve architectural feats. The majestic city of San Lorenzo, the empire's capital, was one of the oldest, if not the oldest, Mesoamerican city. Its sumptuous palaces, temples, and pyramids—the oldest dating back to the first millennium BCE—all were marvels of Olmec engineering. Thanks to a highly sophisticated hydraulic system of pipes, basins, and reservoirs, its inhabitants had access to drinking water.

The layout of the capital was a source of inspiration for builders of many cities thereafter. The Olmecs were also excellent statue sculptors, and their distinctive style inspired several science fiction writers in the twentieth century. Thanks to the drilling and polishing tools they developed, their workshops, and the carrying techniques that they invented to make up for the lack of draft animals and the absence of the wheel, the Olmecs developed a great stone civilization.

They also invented a complex calendar and a writing system and worshiped a number of deities, the most famous of which was undoubtedly the jaguar. Recognized as a symbol of the junction between the earth and the spirit world, the jaguar was represented everywhere in the form of frescoes, sculptures, and engravings on numerous stelae and altar bas-reliefs.

The gigantic and powerful empire followed a hierarchical, ordered system but eventually collapsed. What was the cause of its downfall? It would seem that in the sixth century BCE, the people rebelled against their rulers. In their anger, they destroyed the symbols of power: palaces, temples, and statues of the gods. The revolts, which marked an end to the power embodied by the sovereign, the councilors, and the priests, precipitated the decline and collapse of the Olmec civilization. The ruins of its splendor, buried deep in the jungle, were hidden from sight for a long time.

THE SPARTANS

From the heavens to dust

"When someone wished to know why Sparta didn't have any walls, Agesilaus pointed to the citizens in full armor and said, 'These are the Spartans' walls.'" This famous quote was written by Plutarch in his *Laconic Apothegms*, which expressed, with eloquence, what Sparta symbolized and the fear and respect it inspired in its neighbors. In ancient times, Spartan training, education, and group unity were celebrated and feared both at the Olympic Games and on the battlefield. Sparta, a great rival of Athens, wanted to impose its vision of humankind and strength on the world. Its downfall was all the more dramatic.

In his work *The Description of Greece*, Pausanias was among the first to tell the story of the birth of Sparta: in Laconia, the city-state of Lacedaemon was governed by Lacedaemon, a demigod son of Zeus and Taygete, and husband of Sparta, daughter of Eurotas. It is a fine line between mythology and history, and ancient poets and singers were happy to cross it on numerous occasions: Lacedaemon, or Sparta, as Homer referred to the city, and its inhabitants, the Spartans, triggered the Trojan War.

When did Pausanias's Lacedaemon first emerge? That question remains unanswered. It seems that the city grew considerably during the tenth century BCE and that it was already prosperous when Lycurgus became its legislator two centuries later. By subjecting Spartiates—full citizens of Sparta—to a strict education based on discipline, a spirit of sacrifice, and unfailing obedience to the laws of the city, Lycurgus laid the foundations of a powerful state that, for two centuries, would grow to dominate the entire Peloponnese. Although the first two Persian Wars united the Spartans and Athenians against the Persians, the heavy sacrifices made by the Spartans exacerbated their resentment toward Athens. This led to the outbreak of the Peloponnesian War, which pitted the two cities against each other from 457 to 404 BCE, when Athens surrendered. For more than half a century the Spartans were at the height of their power, cultivating the values that had led to their triumph and glory. However, after having been exposed to the galloping expansion of the Macedonians, soundly defeated by the troops of Alexander the Great at the Battle of Megalopolis in 331 BCE, and battered by the incessant assaults of the Achaean League for two centuries, the Spartans were no more than a shadow of the formidable warriors who had once triumphed over the Athenians when the Romans defeated the Greeks in the first century BCE. When the barbarians invaded Sparta four centuries later, the power and the spirit of sacrifice of its fighters had faded. Only the *Iliad* still had songs for them.

THE ETRUSCANS

....

The cult of sophistication

....

"*Almost the whole of Italy belonged to the Etruscans*," wrote Cato. In the seventh and sixth centuries BCE, a civilization driven by the arts occupied Italy from the Tiber to the Arno and from the peaks of the Apennines to the waves of the Tyrrhenian Sea. The Etruscans developed writing, pottery, goldsmithery, and frescoes depicting lavishly attired musicians and dancers performing for lucky guests at banquets in lush natural surroundings amid garlands of flowers and fruit trees. If the frescoes of the tombs of Tarquinia and Orvieto continue to fascinate and intrigue us today, is it not because they celebrate the opulence and comfortable living of a carefree class?

In the ninth century BCE, peoples from various regions speaking the same language settled around the lakes of northern Italy, where they established the prosperous city-states of the future Etruscan dodecapolis. Over the course of the following century, groups of large villages turned into growing cities and underwent rapid transformations. They gave birth to a civilization that spread throughout what is now the region of Campania and beyond, stimulating trade with neighboring cities. The civilization's elites prospered, as the wealth of treasures found in their tombs can attest.

Etruria reached its peak during the next century, under the reign of Porsenna, the king of Clusium (modern Chiusi). Stretching over part of what is now Latium and Umbria, to the Po River valley in the north and as far south as Campania, Etruria smugly overpowered Rome, then just a small settlement. The Etruscan dodecapolis was a confederation of the most-powerful cities, united around a common religion, ceremonies, rustic performances, horse races, and *ludi*, famous pan-Etruscan games that Rome later adopted, under the authority of the *lucumo*, or ruler. As the many remains that were uncovered can testify, Etruscan society was highly hierarchized. The wine-serving objects and accessories, including craters, oenochoes (wine jugs), canthars, and varnished vases, as well as the rich gold ware, recognizable by the fine granulation of the motifs, used at banquets featuring musical jousting, juggling, and dancing, all bear witness to the opulence of Etruscan

> *In the ninth century BCE, populations from different regions but speaking the same language settled around the lakes in the north of the Italian Peninsula. There they founded the prosperous city-states of the future Etruscan dodecapolis.*

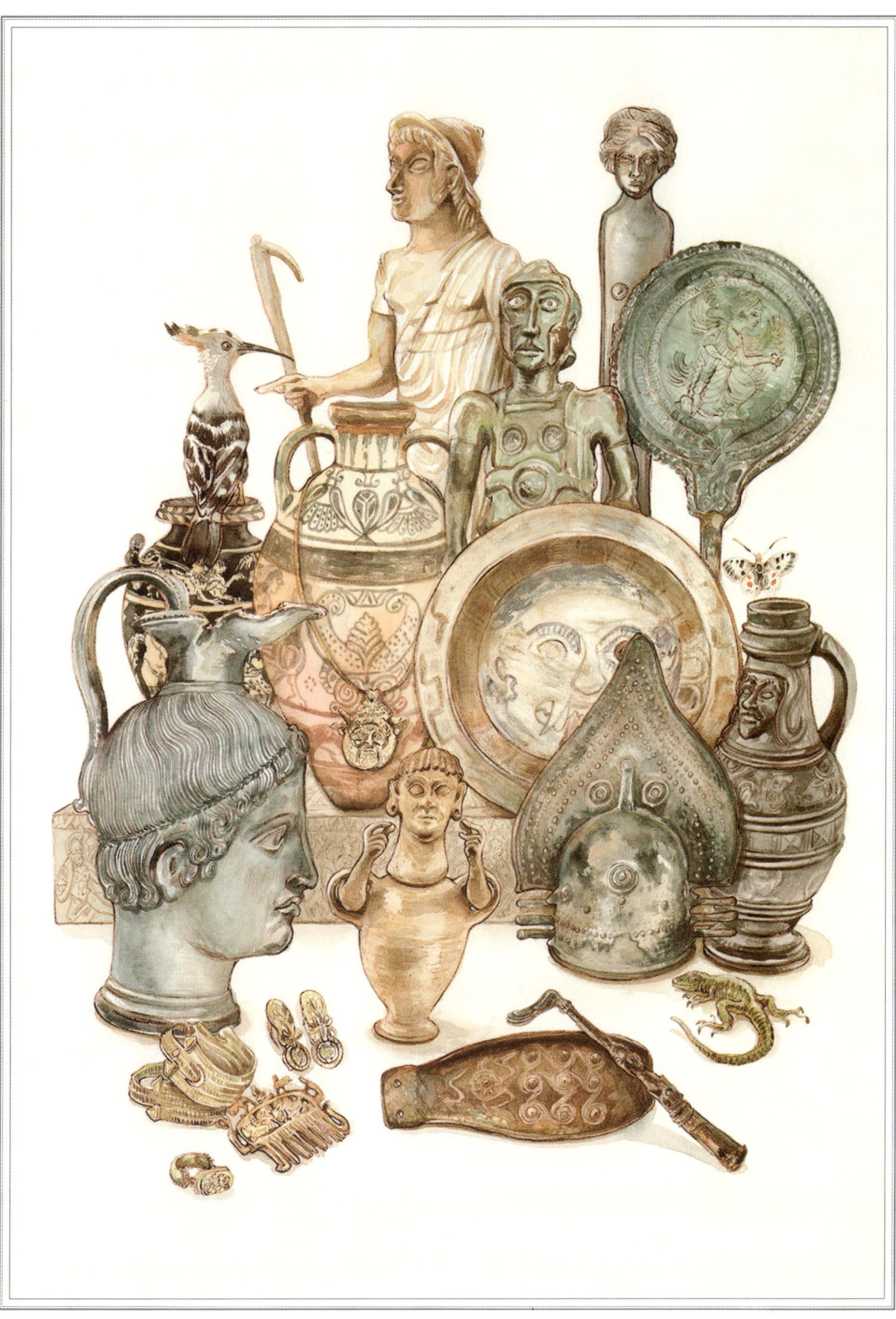

masters. However, trade and crafts also testify to the existence of a wealthy middle class, who flourished thanks to the trade in wine, oil, and ceramics throughout the Mediterranean.

The sixth century BCE was the century of the Etruscans: three Etruscan rulers succeeded each other at the head of Etruria. They were also the first three Roman kings of Etruscan origin. The first of the three, Tarquin the Elder, was praised by Livy (Titus Livius) in *The History of Rome*, Herodotus in the *Histories*, and Dionysius of Halicarnassus in his work *Roman Antiquities*. The Etruscans triumphed everywhere, on land and at sea, most notably against the Phocaeans at the battle of Alalia between 540 and 535 BCE. It was their undivided domination that inspired Cato's famous saying.

Long before Rome, the Etruscan civilization enlightened the Italian Peninsula with its splendor and sophistication, thanks to the influence of its twelve cities. Unfortunately, internal squabbling prevented them from uniting and led to the civilization's downfall. Under the reign of Servius Tullius, Etruria fell into tyranny, weakness, and eventually decadence. Although they won the Battle of Alalia, they were severely defeated in Syracuse and Cumae. They lost control of maritime routes and many trading posts, the use of their language started to fade away (to the benefit of Oscan), and their territory shrank. When the Romans conquered the city of Veii in 396 BCE, it marked the beginning of the end of Etruria. After that conquest the Romans

were unstoppable. In 264 BCE, the capital and last free city of Etruria, Orvieto, was conquered by the Roman Marcus Fulvius Flaccus.

Although its territory fell into Roman hands, the Etruscan civilization lived on thanks to its writings, the last remains of which date back to 50 CE, and above all thanks to its arts, which were remembered by the Italic peoples for centuries. Many Etruscan insignia of power were adopted by the

Long before Rome, the Etruscan civilization enlightened the Italian Peninsula with its splendor and sophistication, through the influence of its twelve cities that were never able to unite.

Romans, including the bronze Capitoline she-wolf that dates back to the fifth century BCE, which gave the city its founding myth. Suetonius recounted that the Roman emperor Claudius wrote a twenty-book history of the Etruscans, praising Rome's Etruscan origins to better cement its greatness. In the fourth century, pan-Etruscan games were organized under the emperor Constantine. And when the Florentine Renaissance rediscovered the Etruscans in the fifteenth century, the Tuscans recognized them as their ancestors. Their origins, way of life, and culture all were intriguing. The Medici claimed to be Etruscan. Their funerary architecture, which mirrored the world of the living, and many Etruscan paintings inspired some of the world's greatest artists, including Leonardo da Vinci and Michaelangelo. It was not until the eighteenth century that serious attempts were made to decipher Etruscan writing and its Greek influence was recognized. Etruscomania was followed by Etruscology, and one discovery followed another. It was revealed that there was not just one dodecapolis, but in fact three, and exchanges with the Hebrews, Lydians, and Egyptians were also documented.

To this day, not all the mysteries of Etruscan writing have been revealed. The anonymous authors of the sacred books that make up the *Etrusca Disciplina* estimated the life span of Etruria at ten centuries. That was more or less how long the civilization lasted.

THE EGYPTIANS

The time of the pharaohs

Of the Seven Wonders of the World, which include the Great Pyramid of Giza, the Hanging Gardens of Babylon, the Statue of Zeus at Olympia, the Temple of Artemis at Ephesus, the Mausoleum at Halicarnassus, the Colossus of Rhodes, and the Lighthouse of Alexandria, only the Great Pyramid of Giza still exists today. The monumental relic belonged to a civilization that enjoyed exceptional longevity: the pharaohs of Egypt.

The oldest signs of human presence in the Nile River valley date to the sixth millennium. However, it was in 3200 BCE that Menes, the very first pharaoh, united the kingdoms of Lower and Upper Egypt, ascended the throne, and inaugurated the first of thirty dynasties. Under the authority of the pharaohs, the priests, and the aristocracy, Egypt developed and flourished around the Nile, whose importance was so great that it was deified under the name Hapi. The river made it possible

for cities to grow alongside it. It also enabled trade and the transportation of goods and materials necessary for the construction of temples and pyramids, which were, and still are, the source of ancient Egypt's splendor and greatness. During its annual flood, the Nile also fostered agricultural development by depositing silt on the surrounding soil. Alongside the farmers, who made up a large part of the population and fed the two kingdoms, ancient Egypt also comprised a considerable proportion of craftsmen and manual workers, who labored dynasty after dynasty to build palaces, temples, necropolises, and pyramids.

Like all civilizations, ancient Egypt alternated between periods of political stability and economic prosperity and periods of unrest and famine. In good times the population led a simple life. The houses unearthed in the towns on either side of the Nile were modest but well furnished. The nobles and the priests led a more agreeable life. The first great pyramids, royal tombs designed to stand the test of time, were built in the third millennium. The most-illustrious examples were the pyramids of Cheops, Chephren, and Mykerinos in Gizeh. Built by the pharaohs that bear their names, they were completed in 2500 BCE. The construction of the pyramids was related to the ancient Egyptians' idea of life and death, according to which the sun, which dies every evening and is reborn the following morning, played a central role. The cult of the dead was based on the belief of resurrecting in a

Like all civilizations, ancient Egypt alternated between periods of political stability and economic prosperity and periods of unrest and famine.

kingdom where life would be eternal. The idea was that only those whose lives and deeds had been remarkable and who were deserving would have access to it. But this idea evolved and made eternal life appear possible for everyone, which had several notable consequences.

To attract the good graces of the gods, and there were many (the Egyptians had more than seven hundred gods and goddesses), the pharaohs had a number of monuments built in their honor, in particular pyramids, each more gigantic than the last, to mark the greatness of their reign. Because their existence in the afterlife had to be as pleasant as their time on Earth, pharaohs and high dignitaries were buried with their furniture, their faithful servants, their wealth, and anything they needed to keep them nourished during the journey into the beyond. Their body was mummified according to a perfectly mastered process and traveled through time to our era in a perfect state of preservation.

Ancient Egypt reached its peak between 1500 and 1000 BCE, with the reigns of illustrious and enlightened sovereigns, both men and women, including Amenhotep, Thutmose, Hatshepsut, Akhenaten, Tutankhamun, Ramses, Seti, and more.

In addition to their remarkable artistic production, ancient Egyptians developed a hieroglyphic script as early as the reign of the first pharaoh, Menes. The complex script was made up of nearly five hundred basic symbols representing sounds or words. The priests used a simplified version of the script. Until the discovery of the Rosetta stone, the hieroglyphic writing of ancient Egyptians remained elusive for a long time, resisting the intuitions and efforts of Egyptologists. The Rosetta stone revealed a text, a decree promulgated by King Ptolemy V in Memphis in the second century BCE, transcribed in hieroglyphics, Demotic, and Greek. It enabled Champollion to finally unlock the mysteries of hieroglyphics in 1822. After this discovery, the Turin King List or the Turin Royal Canon, which provided a precise chronology of the pharaohs who came to the throne during the thirty dynasties that presided over ancient Egypt's destiny, was translated. Over the centuries, the tombs of the Nile valley fell victim to the greed of grave robbers who stole their treasures, depriving archeologists and historians of precious elements to better understand this civilization. The excavation of Tutankhamun's tomb, which had escaped the looters, by British Egyptologist Howard Carter and his team was an unprecedented discovery for our knowledge of this great pharaoh and of ancient Egyptian civilization as a whole. Ancient Egypt and its mysteries were so fascinating that, for a long time, the deaths of Egyptologists who set out to unlock the secret of the pharaohs' tombs were surrounded by curses, and the most-insane hypotheses were put forward to try to explain the location, layout, dimension, and symbolism of the pyramids.

THE ACHAEMENIDS

From riches to rags

Unknown and now forgotten, the Achaemenid Empire's enormous territory was among the largest of its time. In its heyday, from the sixth to the fourth centuries BCE, the empire stretched from the outermost western part of India to the eastern shores of the Mediterranean. In the ninth century BCE, in a region under dispute between the Medes and the Assyrians in the north of modern-day Iran, an ethnic group gained the upper hand over its enemies under the command of its sovereign. Cyrus II, also known as Cyrus the Great, was celebrated by the Scudéry family in their lengthy novels titled *Artamène, or Cyrus the Great*, at the time of Louis XVI.

The accession of Darius in 522 BCE marked a turning point. As a member of the royal guard known as the "ten thousand immortals" and son of the Parthian governor Hystaspes, Darius I, the new king of kings ascended the throne after a coup. He rewrote his ancestry, declaring himself the direct descendant of an enlightened ruler: Achaemenes (which gave birth to the word "Achaemenid"). As soon as he came to power, Darius restored order, kept his enemies in check, repaired the Canal of the Pharaohs, or Necho's Canal, which linked the Red Sea to the Nile and to the Mediterranean, and encouraged the circulation of coins. He reorganized the state, reformed institutions, and built a sumptuous capital, Persepolis, to match his splendor and ambitions. Finally, Darius I sent his armies beyond the limits of his empire to extend his possessions. This gave the Achaemenids unprecedented momentum, which was broken only by the alliance between the fierce Spartans and the brave Athenians in the Greco-Persian Wars. The wars ended with the defeat of the Achaemenid troops in Marathon in 490 BCE.

Xerxes I, Darius's successor, was determined to erase this setback. Ten years later he sacked the city of Athens. But faced with fierce resistance from the Greeks, he was forced to abandon his plans to conquer the Peloponnese. This blow marked the decline of the Achaemenids. Continually plagued by dynastic quarrels, rebellions from its subjugated population, and border attacks, the enormous empire that had brought Asia Minor under its rule was seriously weakened and eventually collapsed. Darius III failed to prevent Alexander the Great from taking the empire's strongholds and its finest architectural monuments. Their colossal ruins, finely sculpted bas-reliefs, gardens, and decors bear witness to what the Achaemenids were like in their heyday when Darius I, "the Great King, the King of Kings, and the King of Countries," claimed to be a descendant of the mythical Achaemenes.

THE PHOENICIANS

The greatest navigators of the ancient world

Praising the Phoenicians' nautical skills, Xenophon has Critobulus say this in a fictitious dialogue with Socrates: *"I once saw, I think, the most beautiful and accurate arrangement of implements possible, Socrates, when I went on board that large Phoenician vessel."* Where did these exceptional sailors come from? In the seventh millennium BCE, the Canaanites settled in what are now Byblos (Lebanon) and Ugarit (Syria). Between 3000 and 2750 BCE they founded several city-states, among which the delightful city of Tyre, and two centuries later they established successful trade relations with the Egyptians. But between 1300 and 1200 BCE, the Canaanites were unable to fight off the expansion of their Aramean, Hebrew, and Philistine neighbors, who destroyed Ugarit, or the assaults of invaders from the sea. They were absorbed into the population and became Phoenicians.

Responding to the call of the sea, the Phoenicians soon proved to be remarkable navigators and set about exploring the Mediterranean coasts, establishing a base in Cyprus, as well as trading posts in North Africa, Sicily, Sardinia, Malta, Corsica, and southern Spain. The Phoenicians also made major contributions to writing by devising an alphabet that later inspired the Greeks to develop their own. Latin, as well as many other alphabetical systems around the world, were derived from the Phoenician alphabet. In 814 BCE, the Phoenicians founded a new city that was destined to an extraordinary fate: Carthage. With its location, its remarkable development, and its trading acumen, the city quickly became a major trading center and a military power that would later make Rome tremble. But from 865 BCE onward, the main Phoenician city-states suffered invasion after invasion and fell under foreign domination. In the seventh century BCE, after the Assyrians, the Phoenicians fell under the dominion of the Babylonians. In the following century, Tyre was reduced to ashes by the Babylonian king Nebuchadnezzar, and the city-states fell under the control of Sidon, and then Persia. In 332 BCE, they fell under the rule of Alexander the Great. At the end of the third Punic War in 146 BCE, Carthage fell too, and in 65 BCE the Romans took over the last Phoenician strongholds. The heyday of this seafaring people had come to an end.

Was the Phoenicians' desire for conquest, and their sense of adventure and exploration, limitless? Did they reach the Azores and the Canary Islands? Did they sail along the west coast of Africa long before the Portuguese? In his work *Histories*, Herodotus reported that Nekao II, the pharaoh who reigned from 610 to 595 BCE, had commissioned Phoenician sailors with the mission to sail around Africa. While it is unlikely that this exploit was actually achieved, the story does speak volumes about the prodigious qualities attributed to Phoenician navigators at the time.

THE AKSUMITES

The first Christians of Africa

It was long described as a gigantic territory inhabited by monstrous beings born of the blistering heat. But beyond the northern region of Barbary, Africa, or the terrae incognitae—lands not yet known, according to the saying *Ex Africa semper aliquid novi*, which translates to "There is always something new out of Africa"—was home to great peoples, civilizations, and kingdoms, the earliest of which was undoubtedly the kingdom of Aksum, or Axum.

In the fourth century BCE, several political entities emerged from the ruins of the kingdom of D'mt on the shores of the Red Sea. By peacefully integrating these entities, the kingdom of Aksum unified the region and then dramatically extended the boundaries of its territory.

What did these peoples live on? Primarily on food derived from agriculture, with wheat and barley growing abundantly thanks to the rich soil, but also from farming and hunting, and above all from trade. In the following century, the Aksumites built ships and ports along the shores of the Red Sea and the Nile, the largest of which was Adulis, to facilitate exchanges in the Mediterranean, the Horn of Africa, Asia, and, notably, India. These exchanges included trade in emeralds, gold, ivory, spices, and silk. With the kingdom's natural wealth, its privileged location at the crossroads of "three worlds," and its commercial activities, Aksum rapidly became a thriving kingdom.

The educated scholars of the kingdom's eponymous capital, built atop the northeastern highlands of present-day Ethiopia, established a language, known as Ge-ez, and its alphabet. The kingdom's craftsmen built monumental constructions, of which the obelisks are the most-famous remains, and the blacksmiths minted coins that were found in the far reaches of the Roman Empire and the great cities and ports of India.

The kingdom found its unity, strength, and stability in a centralized state that was governed with authority and wisdom by a ruling line of enlightened kings, or "Negus." In the third century, King Ezana chose to abandon his polytheistic beliefs and convert to Christianity. What was the reason for this? Legends have it that the Ark of the Covenant, which contained the tablets of the Ten Commandments given to Moses on Mount Sinai, was given by King Salomon to the Queen of Sheba, whose descendants then gifted it to King Ezana. Another legend has it that Ezana converted around the year 340. Either way, one certainty remains: Aksum embraced this new religion and became the first great Christian kingdom of Africa. By this time, the kingdom was at its peak and Aksum was comparable to the Roman Empire, the Persian Empire, and imperial China.

The spread of Islam, the collapse of the kingdom's commercial hegemony, and soil depletion due to overexploitation caused the downfall of the kingdom of Aksum, and none of Ezana's successors were able to prevent its fall. In the tenth century, the deposition of the last sovereign of the Ezana dynasty marked the end of this prestigious kingdom.

THE MOCHE

From influence to oblivion

Of all the pre-Columbian Andean civilizations, the Moche culture was without a doubt among the most brilliant, refined, and wealthy. Paradoxically, this was also a civilization known for the extreme cruelty of its sacrifices. It was on the coast and in the coastal valleys of northern Peru, in a valley where the Moche River flows—hence the civilization's name—that the Moche appeared, at the dawn of our era. From the first to the fourth centuries CE, after defeating their neighbors, the Vicus, Salinar, and Viru cultures, this conquering people, later dubbed the "Greeks of the Andes," extended their territory southward. By consolidating their power in prosperous cities built by ingenious architects, they were able to establish a bona fide empire. These city-states, at the heart of which *huacas* (mud-brick pyramids) were built, formed kingdoms that eventually became empires. The two most famous huacas, Huaca del Sol and Huaca de la Luna, as they were called by the colonists, dominated the main Moche city. At their height in the sixth century, the Moche ruled over a 400-mile territory stretching from the bastion city of Pampa Grande in the north to Pañamarca in the south.

This civilization practiced human sacrifice on a large scale.

The Moche cities were urban centers with administrative and religious functions and possessed pyramids and temples connected by an extensive road network. The Moche society was highly hierarchical. At the head of each city-state—whose population could reach 10,000—was a lord. This lord was also a priest, the most important of all priests, acting as a mediator between men and divinities. He reigned over a caste of warriors and priests under whose authority were craftsmen, peasants, and fishermen. The Moche were skillful farmers who used an ingenious irrigation system to transform the arid expanses of the Peruvian north coast to develop a varied and fertile agriculture. Swept by the El Niño current every winter, the Moche territory was beset by torrential rains. According to archeologists, this harsh climatic environment could explain their warlike nature, their penchant for warfare, and their cruel practices.

One of the aspects of Moche culture that most struck observers and scholars was their cruelty: This civilization practiced human sacrifice on a massive scale. Motifs were uncovered on the frescoes and bas-reliefs of the ceremonial platforms of their monuments that depict their decapitating deity, Ai apaec, which means "the maker," who was also referred to as the "Headsman," with a *tumi*—a sacrificial dagger—in one hand and a decapitated head in the other. Other frescoes suggest that the tortured victims were skinned alive, dismembered, and drained of their blood. Who were the victims? Mainly Moche prisoners from neighboring valleys, captured in local conflicts. The high priests would cut their heads off, and the lords would drink their warm blood to gain the courage and strength of the sacrificed victim. Women and children, as well as concubines and their offspring, also accompanied the slain lords to their grave.

The Moche did not develop a writing system, but they are remembered for their exceptional artistic skills. Thanks to technological improvements borrowed from the peoples they defeated as they expanded their territory, the Moche became excellent craftsmen. They excelled in the production of jewelry, ceramic pottery, metal objects, statuettes—which they produced in large quantities—and frescoes depicting themselves, their domestic animals, and their deities, including Ai apaec, in a variety of scenes from daily life. They also depicted battles among warriors, officiating priests, soldiers torturing prisoners, and mythological creatures.

There are many statuettes and frescoes that show a more cheerful aspect of Moche daily life: sexual encounters. In a variety of unequivocal poses, artists immortalized couples—individuals with identifiable features—in a variety of inventive and explicit poses, enthusiastically indulging in the joys of lovemaking. Their renderings are so realistic and detailed they could make prudes blush . . .

Preserved in the archeological site of Sipán, in today's Lambayeque Province, is the tomb of a second-century nobleman who was discovered adorned with gold jewels. Buried with a child, women, guards, and llamas, he was named "Lord of Sipán" and was probably the governor of the region. Burial platforms decorated with sumptuous frescoes were also unearthed at the site where the bodies of high-ranking Moche dignitaries were laid to rest. The deceased were surrounded with gold objects adorned with precious stones to accompany them on their journey to the other world. While the Moche watched by as their neighbors, the Waris and the Tiwanaku, flourished on their borders, a cataclysm struck the Peruvian coast around the year 600 of our era, engulfing the great Moche cities in earthquakes and floods. Although not all the Moche perished in the catastrophe, their civilization did not recover, and after two centuries of devastation it eventually vanished. Their successors were the refined Incas. Ironically, they too built a brilliant civilization that was to suffer a no-less-spectacular fate.

THE MAYANS

The great mystery

Of all the civilizations, the brilliant and ingenious Mayan civilization remains particularly fascinating today. Undoubtedly, it is because their collapse was among the most dramatic. While several credible hypotheses have been put forward, the enigma remains. Was it an epidemic? A cataclysm? Drought? Maybe a curse? What exactly was, or were, the causes of their disappearance? The Mayans started to settle around the Yucatán Peninsula in the third millennium BCE. They founded their first cities two thousand years before the birth of Christ. Sumptuous city-states named Calakmul, Caracol, and Palenque flourished, and of the hundred or so cities they built, a dozen, such as Tikal, were home to close to 70,000 people. Chichén Itzá was one of the most famous.

The Mayan civilization did not centralize its power. City-states were placed under the authority of a *k'uhul ajaw* (divine lord), who acted as a mediator between men and supernatural forces. His power was partly based on a spectacular display of divine attributes through a host of rituals, ceremonies, and festivities. Over time, a race for prestige and the ostentatious display of wealth, which underlined the sovereign's power, accompanied their formidable rise.

At its pinnacle, at the onset of the sixth century of our era, the Mayan civilization boasted a population nearing ten million inhabitants and comprising members of the elite, priests, craftsmen, warriors, peasants . . . its collapse began around the year 700. The first trigger that led to its collapse was an explosion in its population. The reduced surface area of arable land, combined with poor soils made even poorer by overexploitation, resulted in insufficient yields. To make up for this shortfall, the Mayans converted forests into field, which resulted in full-fledged deforestation. Overexploitation of the newly converted land further depleted the soil. Deficiencies occurred and led to long-lasting famines, undermining the foundations of the powerful empire. Throughout the ninth century, periods of extreme drought plagued the land. Today, geologists believe that this climatic episode also caused the collapse of the Tang dynasty in China at the same time.

The destruction of forests, which drastically reduced the level of humidity transferred from the soil to the atmosphere, was directly responsible for a rise in temperatures ($37°F–41°F$) and a one-third drop in precipitation. The effects were as swift as they were unexpected: the cornfields did not survive these changes.

Its collapse was one of the most dramatic and remains an enigma today.

The city-states' frantic race for prestige and excessive display of wealth, regardless of how it affected what was, in its heyday, the most advanced civilization in all of Mesoamerica, inevitably precipitated the ruin of the urban centers when they faced famine. In an attempt to prevent the collapse, the holy lords ordered their priests to increase the number of ceremonies and human sacrifices performed in honor of Chaac, the god of rain, and Ahmakiq, a god of agriculture. The bloodshed was tremendous, but it was to no avail. The fragility of the city-states, combined with the powerlessness of their sovereigns and priests, gave rise to power struggles and dynastic quarrels among extended royal families. The proliferation of heirs and princes, a result of polygamy, claiming the legitimacy of their power, which they were prepared to take by force of arms, also contributed to precipitating the empire's downfall. The following generation of *k'uhul ajaw* was equally unable to prevent collapse of their cities and the downfall of the empire. With their prayers and sacrifices unanswered, farmers and populations of entire cities lost faith in their rulers and the deities they honored. Throughout the ninth century, they set off in search of less exposed regions more favorable to cultivation.

The Mayan civilization's mortal blow happened after the year 900 and was just as bloody. The desperate lack of resources and fratricidal struggles for power led to military action between the city-states and their populations. The fortified walls, temples, palaces, and buildings destroyed in the fighting bear witness to the unprecedented climate of violence that reigned. Each city-state adopted an individualistic approach and went to war with its neighbors. Each conflict was an opportunity to capture the necessary prisoners for the precious sacrifices required to attract the gods' favors and good graces. The wars that pitted them against each other followed one another at such a pace that populations migrated en masse, leaving behind the power and the quarrels, conflicts, increasingly costly sacrifices, and unproductive supplications they created.

After years of internal turmoil the empire ended its decline in chaos. Taking advantage of the weakness of the city-states and the misguidedness of their rulers, neighboring civilizations, in particular the Toltecs, had no difficulty in striking the final blows to fully destroy a civilization that had so brilliantly illuminated the continent's history.

THE MONGOLS

The people of the steppes

Of all the powers the world has ever known, and excluding Attila's Huns in the fifth century, the Mongols, born in the steppes of central Asia, were probably the most devastating civilization. Yet, nothing seemed to predispose this people to terrorize the globe or to strike fear at the doorstep of Hungarian fortifications and endanger Christianity.

The Mongols are inextricably linked to the environment they flourished in: the Asian steppes. With their bitter-cold winters and scorching summers, the Asian steppes stretch from the farthest reaches of the Orient to the gates of eastern Europe.

The Mongols are inextricably linked to the environment they flourished in. The Asian steppes, endless grasslands that stretch for miles on end, from the farthest reaches of the Orient to the gates of the cities of eastern Europe, are swept by bitter-cold winters and scorching summers. Nomadic pastoralists roamed these plains, moving their camps in search of pasture for their horses and livestock, establishing trade relations with the sedentary peoples they encountered on their travels. Some of these tribes established modest kingdoms, such as the Xianbei in the first and second centuries, or the Rouran Khaganate, who assimilated a considerable number of hordes in the fifth and sixth centuries. Governed by chieftains always eager for more wealth, most of these tribes were belligerent and would attack and pillage villages, appearing and disappearing on their horses in a frenzied whirlwind. Their aim was not to settle in a territory and enslave the local populations; they were just out to make a profit. For decades, the steppes were a scene of constant raids. In the tenth century, the Khitan people gained such momentum that they founded an empire that dominated northern China. They made Beijing one of its capitals until the Song dynasty triumphed over them in the eleventh century. In the second half of the eleventh century, a fatherless child grew up to become the leader of one of these tribes and was instrumental in carving a destiny across the continent for these nomadic riders. The child, who would go on to form the Mongol Empire and transform the destiny of Asia, was called Temüjin. Driven out by his clan, he was condemned to exile. But in 1196, Temüjin was proclaimed ruler, or khan, and in the years that followed he successively defeated the Tatars, the Keraites, and the Naiman, the last of the Mongol people to resist him. He integrated their members

and then dispersed them among the already established Mongol clans and was proclaimed *khagan*, which translates to "supreme ruler," by an assembly of Mongol chiefs in 1206. And so Temüjin became Genghis Khan. In his book the *Life of Saint Louis*, French chronicler Jean de Joinville wrote of the conqueror whose hordes would make the earth shake: "*He said to them: 'Lords, if you want me to be your king, you will swear to me by Him who made heaven and earth that you will obey my commandments.' And they swore it. Then he made provisions to keep the peace amongst the people . . . He made many other good provisions to keep them in peace.*"

With the help of his sons, Genghis Khan defeated the Kyrgyz people and the Oirats in the north, the Uyghurs to the east, and the Tanguts, forcefully subjugating any peoples who refused to peacefully assimilate. For twenty years Genghis Khan considerably expanded the borders of the Mongol

For twenty years, Genghis Khan considerably expanded the borders of the Mongol Empire, destroying everything in his path and retreating after the plunder was over.

Empire, destroying everything in his path and retreating after the plunder was over. In 1215, Genghis Khan led his army into Beijing, and in 1221 they reached the Indus River. When he died in 1227, he was at the head of an empire that was vastly larger than the territories conquered by Alexander the Great. His successors, such as his third son, Ögedei, continued his glorious legacy. From his fortified capital of Karakorum, he launched assaults on the Jin dynasty, in Azerbaijan, and in the South Caucasus. He defeated the Seljuks in Anatolia and clashed with the Song dynasty in China. His grandson Batu, who commanded some 150,000 warriors, further extended the empire's borders. His warriors to the north triumphed over the Bulgarians, the southern hordes defeated the Turks massed between the Volga and the Dnipro Rivers, while the bulk of the hordes, under Batu's command, invaded Russia as far north as Novgorod, despite a heroic resistance. In 1240, the Mongols asserted their control of southern Russia by sacking Kiev. In 1242, just as Batu's armies were about to lay siege to Vienna, Ögedei's death forced him to rush back to the capital to be enthroned as the Great Khan.

Under the brief reigns of Güyük and Möngke, Mongol armies ruthlessly pursued their conquests, invading the Middle East and the Balkans. Their momentum was broken only in 1260, by the Mamluks of Egypt. The defeat may have brought the Mongols' conquests to a halt, but it did not mark

By the end of the fifteenth century, all that remained of an empire that had once been one of the largest in the world were the ruins and desolation left by its warriors in the memories of defeated peoples.

their ruin. That same year, Kublai Khan, the future founder of the Yuan dynasty of China, took power. His arrival heralded a forty-four-year reign that would coincide with the empire's golden age. Under his authority, news and orders were communicated from the capital to the four corners of the empire thanks to a network of roads and postal relays. The empire was connected by two east–west routes: Beijing-Sarai and Kaifeng-Laiazzo, while a river and sea route crossed it from north to south, from the Baltic to Egypt, facilitating the movement of people, goods, and religious doctrines.

Although shamanism was the empire's official religion, the Mongols were tolerant as long as laws were not flouted. Möngke declared, *"We Mongols . . . believe that there is only one God, through whom we have life and through whom we die, and towards him we direct our hearts. . . . But just as God has given the hand several fingers, so he has given mankind several paths."*

The huge empire was fractured into numerous khanates to facilitate its administration. Although Kublai Khan's authority kept the empire together, it began to break up after the death of Abu Sa'id Bahadur Khan. Only the Kipchak Khanate managed to outlast the other khanates, for a century. By the end of the fifteenth century, all that remained of an empire that had been one of the largest in the world in its heyday were the ruins and desolation left by its warriors in the memories of defeated peoples. In his *Compendium of Chronicles*, a comprehensive universal history, Rashid al-Din recalled the bitter words once spoken by Genghis Khan, who foresaw the future downfall and weakening of his people: *"Our descendants will wear gold-embroidered clothing, will eat fat foods and delicate morsels, will ride thoroughbred horses and embrace beautiful women; but they will not say that their fathers and their elder brothers had got these things together for them."*

THE ABBASIDS

The golden age of Islam

In the year 750, a revolution crushed the Umayyad dynasty and ushered Abu al-Abbas al-Saffah to power. As the first caliph of the Arab Muslim Abbasid dynasty, he set about restoring religious authority. Al-Mansur, his successor, continued his work and founded a new capital, Madinat al-Salam (the core of what is today Baghdad), at the heart of the gigantic empire that stretched from North Africa to Transoxania, in lower Asia.

In 786, caliph Harun al-Rashid took the throne. Harun al-Rashid was the second son of al-Khayzuran, a former slave and the favorite wife of his father, al-Madhî. His brother, Musa al-Hadi, briefly preceded him on the throne and probably succumbed to poison. When Harun became caliph, he was given the name al-Rashid, meaning the "rightly guided." As the head of the caliphate, he was skillfully assisted by his vizier, the ambitious Ja'afar al-Barmaki. He entrusted the laborious administration of the empire to his vizier and handled the military affairs himself. Al-Rashid, who was a very pious man, was also *amir al-Mu'minin*, commander of the faithful, and imam, or prayer leader. He strengthened the power around him, fought victoriously against the Byzantines, put an end to the claims of the Barmecides by having them executed, and became famous for the sumptuous gifts he offered King Charlemagne in France, including a splendid elephant praised in the folktales *One Thousand and One Nights*.

Under Harun al-Rashid's reign the caliphate enjoyed administrative, political, and religious stability, as well as an impressive economic development. Craftwork, agriculture, trade with the kingdom of Morocco and the emirate of Córdoba in southern Spain, and unprecedented cultural influence all contributed to the empire's prosperity. Harun al-Rashid, who was himself highly cultured, encouraged the development of the arts. In his sumptuous court he welcomed musicians, storytellers, and, although he was well versed in the religious sciences, poets celebrating the pleasures of life, such as Abu Nuwas: "*Wine is presented to me by a young cupbearer / of the female sex, but dressed as a boy / A tomboy, who mixes genders / and lets herself be loved in two ways / But if one were to mix wine with light / the result would be light upon light.*"

The city of Baghdad was at the height of its glory during the reign of al-Rashid. Tax collectors allowed the caliph and his followers to live in luxury and opulence. But the glory and splendor came at a price. In some parts of the empire, taxes were deemed too high, triggering revolts that Harun al-Rashid ruthlessly put down.

During the last years of his reign, and despite all his efforts, al-Rashid was unable to prevent several emirates and kingdoms, such as those of Córdoba and Morocco, from breaking away from his authority and the caliphate. When he died on an expedition against the rebels of Khorasan in 809, his two sons quarreled, and after four years of war, al-Mamun triumphed over his brother al-Amin. As caliph, he imposed mu'tazilism theology—a combination of Islamic philosophy, rationalism, and logic—as the official school of thought and succeeded, not without difficulty, in establishing his authority.

Despite the troubles that shook the caliphate, this period is remembered in history as the golden age of Islam because of its extraordinary literary, cultural, and artistic influence. Baghdad was a cosmopolitan city home to nearly a million inhabitants, attracting a wealth of scholars, scientists, and artists. Under the impetus of al-Mahdi, and later of Harun al-Rashid, Arab texts were widely circulated and texts from the great Greek thinkers, including major treatises on mathematics, physics, medicine, and astronomy, were translated into Arabic. Baghdad attracted Persians, Indians, and Chinese, all of whom contributed their knowledge to the caliphate's extraordinary influence.

Due to the vastness of the territory and the remoteness of its borders, power eluded the caliphs, but this did not profoundly affect the empire at first. In 945, caliph al-Mustakfi delegated his power to the Turkish Buyid dynasty. After two centuries of adversity, the caliphate regained its power and glory thanks to Saladin, the founder of the Ayyubid dynasty, who spearheaded the military effort of the Abbasid caliphate, faithfully and diligently leading the counter-crusade. His death in 1193 was the beginning of the caliphate's final period of decline. In 1258, Hulagu's Mongol hordes ravaged Baghdad and marked the end of the Abbasid caliphate.

The legacy of a radiant caliphate, and the most brilliant of the caliphs who ruled it, Harun al-Rashid, lives on through the enchanting folktales of *One Thousand and One Nights*. Many of these tales, such as *The Tale of Caliph Harun al-Rashid and the False Caliph*, celebrate the ruler, who is often portrayed in disguise as he mingles with the common people: "*It is related that the Caliph Harun al-Rashid was one night restless with extreme restlessness, so he summoned his Vizier Ja'afar the Barmacide, and said to him: 'My breast is straitened and I have a desire to divert myself to-night by walking about the streets of Baghdad and looking into folks' affairs; but with this precaution that we disguise ourselves in merchants' gear, so none shall know us.'*" Rumor has it that on certain nights, when the moon is full, the caliph's shadow still wanders through the alleyways of what remains of the glorious city of Baghdad.

Baghdad was a cosmopolitan city home to nearly a million inhabitants, attracting a wealth of scholars, scientists, and artists.

THE KHMERS

Masters of stone carving and water

At the very end of the eighth century CE in present-day Cambodia, the ruler Jayavarman II defeated the local overlords who ruled the region's fiefdoms, crushed any resistance, and founded a kingdom that he built around him by proclaiming himself *chakravartin* (god-king). His successors, Jayavarman III and Indravarman I, continued his policies and contributed to the kingdom's development by building important temples. In 1145, after long periods of unrest due to incessant dynastic squabbles, the warrior king Suryavarman II ordered the construction of the temple of Angkor Wat, dedicated to the god Vishnu, in the city of Yashodharapura.

For nearly forty years, thousands of workers labored on this masterpiece dedicated to the deity of Khmer rulers. They carved and sculpted its bas-reliefs depicting the deeds of legendary heroes and the graceful movements of hundreds of apsara dancers, water-protecting nagas, and earth genies. For generations to come, this is where the Khmers would worship the first of the god-kings.

For nearly forty years, thousands of workers labored on this masterpiece dedicated to the deity of Khmer rulers: Angkor Wat.

Mountain temples, called as such in honor of Mount Meru, the cosmic mountain and mythical home of Khmer gods, were built throughout the kingdom. Over the years, a sprawling city with a complex hydraulic network that must have covered almost 620 square miles and wooden, bamboo, and straw dwellings that have since disappeared developed around this temple. For three centuries the Khmers honored their king, as well as Vishnu and Shiva. Indian deities also joined the pantheon of local divinities, since religious tolerance encouraged and protected the expression of countless cults. During this period the Khmer kingdom extended throughout Southeast Asia and prospered under the authority of its ruling god-king, with the support of Brahmins and a powerful aristocracy.

In the twelfth century, Mahayana Buddhism became the official religion. Under the reign of Jayavarman VII, the "great city" of Angkor Thom was chosen as the kingdom's capital and became one of the largest. With a population of some 250,000 inhabitants, it was also one of the most densely populated cities of its time. Angkor Thom was surrounded by thick walls and monumental gates, each adorned with the face of one of the four rulers of the Hindu pantheon, and at its center proudly stood the temple of Bayon, where fifty-four gigantic towers rose into the skies. Zhou Daguan, a Chinese diplomat, witnessed processions that took place here, and wrote in his report *The Customs of*

Cambodia around 1300: "*When the king goes out, troops lead the escort; then come flags, banners, and music.*" Like him, many travelers expressed their admiration for the number of hospitals, shrines, guesthouses, and rich libraries scattered throughout the kingdom.

In the fourteenth century, Theravada Buddhism replaced Mahayana Buddhism. For decades the Khmers had developed an extensive network of roads: they cut endless paths through abundant vegetation and built bridges across rivers to connect the kingdom's cities. To contain the devastating monsoon floods and prevent them from engulfing and submerging the city of Angkor, the Khmers constantly designed and perfected gigantic, ingenious hydraulic networks including pipes, basins, dikes, and reservoirs, capturing water from floods and releasing it during the terrible months of drought to irrigate crops and provide drinking water. Engineers, builders, craftsmen, and workers spared no effort to tame the hostile natural environment. So how did this flourishing and lavish civilization collapse?

During the fourteenth and fifteenth centuries, there were two thirty-year periods when severe monsoon instability shook the kingdom. The king, along with the court and elites, left Angkor for Phnom Penh. They were soon followed by the entire population. It would seem that the Khmers were no longer able to keep water under control.

The cities that were a testimony of the greatness of Khmer civilization before the kingdom imploded and fell into disuse and oblivion, as if no one had ever lived there. Over the next centuries, Angkor Thom, Angkor Wat, and countless other vestiges of Khmer civilization were swallowed up by the jungle, and their stones became covered in moss under a tangle of lianas. It was not until 1861, when this kingdom, which had since been renamed Cochinchina, began to be explored by antiquities enthusiasts, adventurers, and scholars, that two Frenchmen, naturalist Henri Mouhot and Father Sylvestre, unearthed these marvelous stone monuments. The two men were among the first to try to uncover the secret behind the collapse of the brilliant civilization that had built them.

A series of missions were able to reveal the wonders of a civilization praised by writers. French writer Pierre Loti celebrated the "masks" of the Bayon, and Paul Claudel was fascinated by the apsaras "with their Ethiopian smile, dancing a kind of sinister cancan over the ruins." In 1926, as he returned from Asia, Paul Morand brought back in his luggage a relic of this thousand-year-old civilization: one of those Buddha heads that Chinese antique dealers would come to offer him in secret, at night, "*rolled up in cloths like a severed head.*"

THE VIKINGS

The conquerors of the North

These proud conquerors of the North, whose origins go far back, sailed up rivers to raid the Atlantic coasts and were the first to make contact with Native Americans. At the dawn of the Carolingian era, they set out to conquer the seas on their *skeids*. The mere sight of these ships caused horror and desolation.

The Vikings, who were also referred to as the Nortmanni (men of the North), were fishers, traders, and outstanding carpenters. They descended from people who sailed across Scandinavia in rudimentary boats and developed a civilization on the Scandinavian coasts in a hostile environment.

After the ice melted, the northern lands were covered with moss, then with dense forests. The people who came to be known as the Nortmanni (men of the North) were descendants of peoples who sailed across Scandinavia in rudimentary boats. They were fishers, traders, and outstanding carpen-

ters and developed a civilization along the Scandinavian coasts in a rather hostile environment. Four thousand years before the birth of Christ, they settled, and a millennium later they had mastered bronze work and were producing artfully crafted weapons, tools, clothing, and jewelry.

The Vikings worshiped divinities who were themselves dominated by two main gods: Odin, the god of war, and Thor, the god of thunder. The existence and the destiny of the Vikings changed when they set out beyond their cold shores. The effects of a harsh climate in an extreme environment, rapid population growth, lack of arable land, and what appears to have been countless clan feuds were the reasons for their departures and incursions. But the Vikings had been sailing across icy waters long before then. Their first major raid is thought to have taken place in 793, when they reached the island of Lindisfarne at the northeastern tip of England. They plundered its monastery and returned each year to sow death on a different island or city. Viking boats, the famous *skeids* or *knörrs*—incorrectly called *drakkars*—were very maneuverable and enabled them to navigate both the high seas and shallow waters, rivers, and streams, using sails and oars.

Trade routes close to their coasts sparked interest in the Vikings. For three centuries they traveled, raided neighboring islands and lands, and forged their national identities, later becoming the Swedes, Danes, and Norwegians. From the

early ninth century onward, Vikings from Sweden traveled up the Volga and the Dnipro Rivers deep into Russia, where they helped found Kiev and Novgorod. Under their rule these cities became renowned for trade and the arts. The Persian explorer Ibn Rustah wrote of them: *"They live exclusively from trade with the Slavic country."* Hungry for fruit, spices, wine, jewelry, and silks, they made their way to Constantinople. Miklagard, or "the great city" as they called it in their language, is where the strongest of them formed an elite guard serving the Byzantine emperors.

In 839, under the command of Thorgis, the Vikings conquered the north of Ireland and founded a settlement called Dyflin, which later became Dublin. Norwegians and Danes clashed for control of the island, but it was not until the year 1000 that the Irish chieftain Brian Boru triumphed, driving out the invaders and proclaiming himself king. Al-

For three centuries the Vikings traveled, raided neighboring islands and lands, and forged their national identities, later becoming the Swedes, Danes, and Norwegians.

though they were unable to conquer Ireland, the Vikings took advantage of the quarrels between rival clans to settle along the coast and helped found the cities of Waterford, Wexford, Wicklow, and Limerick.

At the beginning of the second half of the ninth century, Vikings from Denmark and Norway began to attack the dwindling cities of the Carolingian Empire, weakened by the deaths of Charlemagne and Louis the Pious. Their progress was meteoric. They swept through two prosperous trading centers, Dorestad and Hamburg, as well as Rouen, Chartres, Tours, Nantes, and Bordeaux. Finally, they sailed up the Seine to lay siege to Paris, but the fortified city put up such stiff resistance that they were unable to capture it.

The year 911 marked a turning point in the Vikings' conquests. The Viking warlord Rollo and the French king Charles III, called the Simple, signed the Treaty of Saint-Clair-sur-Epte, which granted Rollo control of lands along the lower Seine, the Duchy of Normandy, and the eastern part of the French kingdom in exchange for his loyalty. The Vikings became Normans and settled down. Their way of life and laws adapted. Viking culture and Christian society blended, and the men of the North began to convert to Christianity.

The Vikings also settled in Iceland, the Faroe Islands, and Greenland. Erik the Red was credited for giving Greenland its name in 982. But the resources the island offered soon proved insufficient, and from there they launched their *skeids* across the Atlantic and reached the American continent. In their epic poems they named the American continent Vinland. They set up camp on the coasts and came into contact with the natives, whom they named *skraelings*, or "barbarian." The stormy relations between them explain why they did not progress farther inland.

Beyond the Scandinavian countries, parts of their language, culture, and traditions are still alive in Brittany, Ireland, England, and Scotland.

During the following century, King Cnut the Great founded the North Sea Empire, bringing together Norwegians, Danes, and the English, following the conquest of northern England. At the same time, the Shetland Islands, the Hebrides, and a large part of Scotland also fell to the Vikings. The advent of the second half of the tenth century marked the beginning of the great Norman conquests under the leadership of William the Conqueror. In 1066, following the Battle of Hastings, the Normans conquered a large part of England and Sicily, which they were to rule for three decades, and which would be among the island's most glorious periods.

The Vikings excelled in agriculture, trade, and naval engineering. In addition to their prose stories and histories, called *sagas*, they produced a rich variety of arts and crafts of great finesse. Beyond the Scandinavian countries, parts of their language, culture, and traditions are still alive in Brittany, Ireland, England, and Scotland. On their journeys the Vikings visited lands far from their bases, where they settled or set up camp before setting sail again to explore other river or sea routes . . .

THE GOKOMERE PEOPLE

The end of a nation of builders

It was in the fifth century that the Gokomere, a group of farmers and iron craftsmen of Bantu origin in central Africa, settled in the area where the city of Great Zimbabwe would grow and prosper. The valleys and hills of the region were rich in gold, and over the course of five centuries the Gokomere perfected various mining techniques and produced a plethora of objects from precious metal. They were an industrious and refined people, producing shimmering fabrics, splendid ceramic jewelry, and sculptures in steatite, a very soft rock.

Surprisingly, it was their tremendous prosperity that precipitated their downfall.

From the tenth to the thirteenth centuries, the Gokomere built the imposing stone city of Great Zimbabwe (near modern-day Masvingo), erecting and assembling stone buildings without mortar. Protected by granite ramparts and with a population of up to 20,000, the city was ruled by a sovereign and an aristocracy. It was home to skillful craftsmen and inspired artists who forged trade links throughout the Horn of Africa and as far as the Far East via the ports of Kiloa and Sofala, exchanging their ivory and gold for copper objects, silks, and pearls.

Until the end of the fourteenth century, the kingdom lived in peace and prosperity. Paradoxically, the Gokomere did not collapse as a result of the exactions and plundering of the European colonists. They disappeared even before the Portuguese arrived on the Dark Continent. Surprisingly, it was their tremendous prosperity that precipitated their downfall. Faced with a galloping birthrate lasting several decades, the kingdom was unable to stem the depletion of its resources, which led to an unprecedented famine and triggered revolts both inside and outside the walls. As a result the kingdom imploded, with neither the sovereign nor his aristocracy able to prevent its rapid collapse.

In the city of Great Zimbabwe, many families who had lived in opulence were forced into exile to escape popular persecution. Among those who migrated north, the royal Nyatsimba Mutota founded the kingdom of Mutapa. European conquerors and explorers called it Monomotapa, and the kingdom's resources—cotton, iron, and copper, but above all, gold—would sustain their dreams of wealth.

When the German explorer Karl Mauch and his expedition discovered the gigantic walls of the city of Great Zimbabwe in 1871, they were so amazed by their height, configuration, and splendor that they thought they were looking at the ruins of the palace of the legendary Queen of Sheba in the magnificent city of Ophir.

THE RAPA NUI

Facing the stars

What led people to settle on this desolate island, which they named Rapa Nui, stranded miles from everything, with its inhospitable coastline and sparse vegetation? Why, in honor of what deities or for what miracles, did they build gigantic statues carved out of volcanic tuff with the strength of their wrists, using rudimentary stone tools? Why did these people of the Pacific tip the gigantic statues into pits after they built them, or erect them at the cost of unimaginable effort on top of the sanctuaries dedicated to their ancestors? These "tall, monstrous statues, the work of some now-vanished race," as Pierre Loti later described them, continue to puzzle us today.

From their origins and nautical journeys to their collapse, these argonauts have an unusual history that began around 1500 BCE. At the time, seafaring peoples with an extraordinary knowledge of the winds, currents, and stars sailed across the western Pacific in search of new lands aboard gigantic sailing vessels. During the first millennium they undertook journeys spanning thousands of miles that brought them to Hawaii, the present-day Marquesas Islands, and what became Rano Raraku. Having brought with them yams, taros, sweet potatoes, and tree seedlings, as well as dogs, pigs, chickens, and rats, these intrepid navigators were the first inhabitants and, in the collective memory, are remembered as gods for having brought life's necessities to the island. Their glorious memory has been handed down from generation to generation in Maori songs. The highly hierarchical society developed under the authority of a king whose power derived from *mana*, the creative energy inherited from his ancestors. The society was composed of nobles, priests, craftsmen, and slaves whose existence was marked by the construction of *moai* (statues of the gods or deified ancestors), the building of fast boats (the longest of which could reach 100 feet), crop cultivation, and herding. Early on, the island was divided into clans or *mata*, comprising several families. Each had its own *aku*, a place of worship and burial that was guarded by a moai. The islanders' pantheon was particularly rich. No fewer than ninety divinities were identified, and the most important was Makemake, the very first God, often depicted in the form of a man with a bird's head.

And this was how life went by for more than half a millennium, as if frozen in time.

These "tall, monstrous statues, the work of some now-vanished race," as Pierre Loti later described them, continue to puzzle us.

In his search for a land that had been sighted some twenty years earlier by Edward Davis, the Dutch navigator Jacob Roggeveen landed on Easter Island in April 1722. Since he had landed on the island during the Easter celebrations, he gave it the name Paasch Eylandt, or Easter Island. The encounter be-

Throughout the eighteenth century, navigators sailed by Easter Island, and with them came scientific expeditions that stopped to contemplate the stone giants and try to unravel their mystery.

tween the Europeans and the natives, described by the former as promiscuous petty thieves, was initially euphoric but then turned bloody. Following a misunderstanding, ten islanders were killed. After much discussion, harmony was restored, and on April 10, Jacob Roggeveen set sail again in search of the southern continent. Unfortunately, this sad incident was only the first in a series of misunderstandings and unfortunate episodes between the islanders and their visitors, which were to shed more blood on the island each time.

Throughout the eighteenth century, navigators sailed by Easter Island, and with them came scientific expeditions that stopped to contemplate the stone giants and try to unravel their mystery. In 1774, James Cook set foot on the island. Observing that nature had been "*so sparing of her favors to this spot,*" he was struck by the resemblance between the Rapa Nui and the peoples he had already encountered and concluded that it was the "*same race [that had] spread over all the islands of this vast ocean.*" In 1786, Jean-François de Galaup, comte de Lapérouse, made a stopover there with his ships *L'Astrolabe* and *La Boussole*: "*There is no one who, having read the reports of the last voyagers, can take the Indians of the South Sea for savages,*" he wrote. "*On the contrary, they have made great progress in civilization, and I believe them to be as corrupt as they can be relative to the circumstances in which they find themselves: my opinion on this is not based on the various thefts they committed, but on the way they went about them. The most shameless rascals in Europe are less hypocritical than these islanders.*" His stopover marked the end of the great scientific expeditions of the Enlightenment.

In the very beginning of the nineteenth century, the island was once again the object of much envy. The Rapa Nui fell victim to violent raids by whalers and unscrupulous adventurers. They had become so distrustful that in 1816, Russian admiral Otto von Kotzebüe, whose intentions were peaceful, was greeted with stones thrown at him. In the second half of the nineteenth century, the island was struck by an unprecedented tragedy. In 1862, Peruvian slave traders decimated the population, wiping out half of the island's one thousand inhabitants. Six survivors, infected with smallpox and tuberculosis, contaminated the rest of the island. There were only six hundred inhabitants when the first missionary arrived in 1864. But the island's destruction was not yet complete. In 1868, Jean-Baptiste Onésime Dutrou-Bornier, who wanted to make the island a French protectorate by force, unleashed hell on the island before he was murdered. Julien Viaud, alias Pierre Loti, a young naval cadet, visited the island four years later and wrote in his notebooks: "*Rapa Nui is the name by which the natives refer to Easter Island—and in the very sound of that name I hear echoes of sadness, savagery, and the darkness of night. . . . The darkness of time, the darkness of the island's origins or the darkness of the sky—it is unclear what kind of darkness is implied.*" By then the inhabitants were nothing more than ghosts of the glorious Rapa Nui who had once constructed the *moai*.

For a long time, these gigantic statues with their eyes turned toward the stars were a source of great fascination. They even gave rise to the wildest hypotheses. The whimsical Erich von Däniken wrote in his equally amusing book *Chariots of the Gods*: "*An orally transmitted legend tells us that flying men landed and lit fires in ancient times. The legend is confirmed by sculptures of flying creatures with big staring eyes.*" To put it more plainly, the history and culture of the Rapa Nui have yet to reveal all their secrets. For example, the origin, age, and meaning of the *rongorongo*, wooden tablets covered with writings and anthropomorphic and zoomorphic signs, remain a mystery to this day.

For a long time, these gigantic statues with their eyes turned toward the stars were a source of great fascination. They even gave rise to the wildest hypotheses.

THE SONGHAI

The last of the great African empires

In the seventh century, under the rule of Faran Maka Bote, the small village of Kukiya, in the loop of the Niger River, became the birthplace of the Songhai kingdom. Songhai experienced a remarkable expansion and became one of Africa's most important kingdoms in just a few decades. This was due to the fruitful relations its merchants forged with the kingdoms of the North, notably Morocco, which lasted for centuries, where they sold various commodities: ambergris, gum, salt, slaves, and gold in exchange for cereals, fabrics, weapons, and jewelry.

At the end of the seventh century, the Dia rulers seized power and kept it for six centuries. Around the year 1000, King Kossoi converted to Islam, and all his people followed. The kingdom took the name Songhai, and the sovereign and his court set-

In the seventh century, Songhai underwent a remarkable expansion and became one of Africa's most important kingdoms in just a few decades, thanks to the fruitful relationships its merchants forged with the kingdoms of the North.

tled in the new capital, Gao, along the river Niger. Not so far was a humble city that would eventually overshadow Gao: the city of Timbuktu. With routes reaching as far as Northwest Africa via the Tuat region and as far as Egypt through the Hoggar Mountains in the south of the Sahara Desert, Timbuktu would become one of the most important trading centers in the Sahara. Timbuktu was the kingdom's economic hub, as well as its religious and intellectual center, and it would continue to inspire European explorers for centuries. The rapidly expanding city soon welcomed the construction of adobe buildings and majestic mosques. In the twelfth century, following the conquest of Sudan by the Almoravids, Gao became Muslim for several decades. Eager to extend its influence and the limits of its territory, the powerful Mandinka Empire of Mali set about conquering Songhai, which fell partly under its control.

The Sonni dynasty emerged around the year 1275. At the very end of the thirteenth century, Ali Kolen, a prince who had been taken into slavery, managed to escape, and when he returned to his homeland he founded the second Songhai Empire in Gao in 1335. In 1402, Anselme d'Ysalguier, a French knight and adventurer from the city of Toulouse, is said to have reached the city and married a Songhai princess. Eight years later he returned with her to Occitania, in southwestern France, praising the splendor of the Songhai court and the greatness of this empire, which was still largely unknown to Europe.

Under the reign of Ali Kolon, later known as Sonni Ali and Ali the Great, Songhai freed itself from the Malian Empire's grip and triumphed over the Fulani and Tuareg people. Ali the Great extended the kingdom's borders, capturing Timbuktu in 1468 and Djenné in 1473, making Songhai a threatening neighbor to the Mandinka Empire. His successor, Muhammad Ture, was the first ruler of the Askia dynasty. Upon his return from a pilgrimage to Mecca, he converted the kingdom to Islam with a degree of violence that had never been seen before. He extended the kingdom's borders as far as the Senegal River, placing the conquered territories under Islamic influence, made them prosperous, and turned Gao and Timbuktu into major religious and intellectual centers where doctors, jurists, and scholars exchanged ideas. In 1507, Leo Africanus visited Songhai—which he called the "land of the Black people"—and wrote glowing accounts of the region in books I and VII of his *Description of Africa*. At the height of its glory, the Songhai Empire covered a gigantic territory from Senegal to the loop of the Niger. Its downfall, fueled by dynastic quarrels, was all the more brutal.

Covering a gigantic territory from Senegal to the Niger bend, the Songhai Empire was at its peak.

In 1529, Askia Muhammad was overthrown by his son, Musa. Over the next decade, corruption set in until Daoud, another of Muhammad's sons, dethroned Musa. Daoud restored royal authority, made the Songhai Empire a power in West Africa once again, revived the trade with Morocco that had faltered with his predecessors, and reestablished diplomatic relations with Sultan Ahmad IV el-Mansur. By the time he died in 1589, the Songhai had regained their power and glory. But harmony did not outlive him for long.

Envious of his neighbor's wealth and eager to claim it for himself, the sultan sent an army of mercenaries to the desert of Taghaza in Songhai, in 1589. He then sent a second army of three thousand men the following year, after the first had been overcome by heat and thirst. The Songhai ruler Ishaq II, whose armies were far superior in numbers, was defeated by the thousand men who survived the desert crossing. The muskets and arquebuses of the military leader Judar Pasha's troops overwhelmed the rudimentary weapons of Ishaq II's infantry and cavalry. After retreating, Ishaq II made a substantial peace offer. But the sultan was confident that he had the advantage and the strength and declined. His armies showed no mercy. They crushed the troops of the Songhai Empire at Tondibi in 1591. As he fled, Ishaq II fell to the rebels. With the last pockets of resistance reduced to nothing, Judar Pasha triumphantly marched into Gao before moving on and settling in the more flamboyant city of Timbuktu. The Songhai Empire was no more, and with it disappeared the last of the great African empires. On April 20, 1828, Frenchman René Caillié finally arrived in Timbuktu, the city forbidden to Christians, wearing a burnous and inspired by the writings of medieval Arab travelers. At first he was filled with great happiness: "*As I entered this mysterious city, which had been the subject of research by the civilized nations of Europe, I was struck by an indescribable feeling of satisfaction; I had never experienced such a sensation and my joy was extreme.*" But this was without taking into account the disappointment he felt when he entered Timbuktu: "*I had formed an entirely different idea of the splendor and wealth of this city. At first glance, it is nothing but a mass of poorly built mud houses. In every direction, all you can see are immense plains of shifting sand, white to yellow in color, and extremely arid.*" As though to offset his disillusion, he tempered his remarks and added, "*Nevertheless, there is something impressive about seeing such a large city rising in the middle of the dunes, and the founders' efforts can only be commended.*" Nothing remained of the rich, prosperous, and intoxicating city described by the Arabs. The author and traveler Paul Morand was to follow in the footsteps of so many others and discovered the city a century after René Caillié. He passed his own final judgment in his journal *Paris-Timbuktu*, which retraced his African journey: "*Where are the gleaming domes, the sacks of gold dust and the ivory of the caravans that you read about? . . . A lifeless landscape, bleached by a sun that has gone mad. Timbuktu, once a city of over a hundred thousand people, is now a village of just five thousand. Invaded by the desert,*

Nothing remained of the rich, prosperous, and intoxicating city described by the Arabs.

bloated with gunpowder, covered in sand, rolled into a cone by the cold nights, swollen by the heat, cracked by temperature variations, built with perishable materials, it is falling into ruin and no longer has any strategic or commercial importance." Timbuktu had long been nothing more than a mirage.

THE PITCAIRN ISLANDERS

An inevitable demise

Pitcairn is a small volcanic island in the Pacific. It is far from maritime routes, five days by canoe from Mangareva Island and one from Henderson Island. It has nothing of the enchanting paradise islands with their warm colors, luxurious vegetation, and abundant wildlife. Or rather, it no longer has all this. Pitcairn, like the neighboring islands, was once a fertile land with an abundance of natural resources and forests, and soils suitable for cultivation. Trade made up for any shortfalls. And although these resources dwindled, the island retained enough assets to attract and maintain a population.

Who were the island's first inhabitants? Polynesians. Where did they come from? Most likely from the Marquesas Islands or the Society Islands. They must have discovered the island during their explorations that took them as far as the Hawaiian Islands and Rapa Nui. When did they settle there?

Their society would slowly and tragically collapse, disintegrating over the next five centuries as they struggled to survive in an environment and in conditions that became more challenging with each passing season.

Around the year 800 of our era. For two centuries the population grew and prospered, at peace with its neighbors. Although there was an abundance of resources at first, they were eventually barely sufficient to meet the needs of the islanders. Little did they know that their society would slowly and tragically fall apart over the next five centuries, as they struggled to survive in an environment and in conditions that became more testing with each passing season.

Around the year 1000, the island's population was at its peak, with no more than one hundred inhabitants. The sparsely wooded island was crisscrossed by rivers but not very suitable for cultivation. The absence of a coral reef made fishing and shellfish gathering difficult, so the islanders made do with their only resource: oysters. In a hostile environment where survival was the daily concern, the Pitcairn Islanders fashioned tools from oystershells and stones. These were genuinely their true assets. Although their tools were rudimentary, they enabled the islanders to establish fruitful exchanges with the inhabitants of the neighboring Mangareva Island, swapping them for pigs, bananas, and taros. But it was with the inhabitants of Henderson Island, an island surrounded by a coral reef, that the Pitcairn Islanders established the most-fruitful exchanges. Henderson islanders provided them with tubers, fruit, fish, shellfish, turtle eggs, birds, and feathers of parrots and red-tailed tropical birds, which they used as splendid ornaments for

ceremonial cloaks. Mangareva is the westernmost of the three islands. Located 930 miles east of the Society Islands and southeast of the Marquesas Islands, Mangareva was also the richest of the three, with its sweet potatoes, yams, banana trees, breadfruit trees, and black-lip pearl oysters.

Because only a small number of families were able to survive on the island, Pitcairn Islanders took wives from Mangareva and Henderson to overcome endogamy and incest. The Pitcairn Islanders could not have survived without these interisland exchanges. According to archeologists, the civilization lasted five centuries. After the year 1500 there were no more traces of them. What happened?

Archeologists do not rule out the possibility that the inhabitants of Mangareva resorted to cannibalism to survive.

Deforestation destroyed the island's fragile economy. Flora and fauna withered away. Without enough trees to make their canoes, they were unable to catch enough fish or continue trading with neighboring islands. Many islanders took a final voyage to settle on Mangareva or Henderson. Those who did not leave Pitcairn for good did not survive

long. The barren lands dedicated to cultivating a few miserable crops were unable to yield much produce, hunting and rats had devastated several species of seabirds and land birds, and the shellfish along the shores had practically disappeared due to intensive consumption. The last Pitcairn Islanders soon died out, and the island became deserted. What could have been a mere epiphenomenon actually had disastrous consequences. Since Pitcairn, Henderson, and Mangareva all were dependent on each other for their survival, the demise of the Pitcairn Islanders precipitated the collapse of the fragile societies of Henderson and Mangareva.

The inhabitants of Henderson Island struggled to survive without the regular visits they received and, above all, the tools bought from the Pitcairn Islanders. There were not enough trees to build boats capable of navigating the high seas, so they were forced to adapt. They used giant clamshells as hatchets; bird bones as awls; and pieces of limestone, coral, and clamshells as baking stones and carved the oystershells they found, instead of the sturdy black-lip pearl oystershells, to make rudimentary hooks. Thanks to these ingenious alternatives, they were able to survive the end of trade with Pitcairn Islanders for another century at best. How then did they disappear? Was it because of a natural catastrophe? Did an unfair distribution of the island's last resources lead to a deadly conflict? Cannibalism? Mass suicide? Famine? To this day their disappearance remains a mystery. There is only one certainty: when British navigator Philip Carteret arrived on Henderson in 1606, the island was also deserted.

Only Mangareva, the largest of the three islands and the core of the trade network, was still sparsely populated when James Wilson visited in 1797. Nonetheless, it too had suffered from the collapse of the two neighboring islands. The end of trade with Pitcairn and Henderson and the ensuing lack of resources led to conflicts between families that escalated into bloody wars. Archeologists do not rule out the possibility that the inhabitants of Mangareva resorted to cannibalism to survive.

Seven years prior to Wilson's arrival in 1797, a group of mutineers led by the impetuous Fletcher Christian, who had dared to defy and humiliate Captain Bligh on his vessel HMS *Bounty*, took refuge on Pitcairn Island to escape the verdict of death by hanging that awaited them. There they found traces of a distant human presence. For generations the mutineers and their descendants struggled to survive. Had they been cursed for their crime? The island's current inhabitants, who still cling to the island and their extraordinary history, are mostly descendants of these mutineers.

THE AZTECS

"Sun, god of fire . . ."

Who were the Aztecs' most distant ancestors? Where and when did they appear? In the codices that were spared from the fires, the pages that recount their origins, the wars they fought, and their rather obscure, allegorical migrations have given rise to a variety of interpretations. One thing is certain: during the first millennium BCE, different peoples fought ceaselessly to eclipse their rivals and dominate the Mexican Altiplano in the highlands of central Mexico.

After bitter battles the Totonacs triumphed, and, around 300 BCE, these remarkable builders, descendants of the Olmecs, set about constructing a gigantic city, the largest ever built. By 200 BCE, Teotihuacán, the "city of the gods," was complete. It seems that the city reached its heyday around the same time the Roman Empire collapsed.

The famous prophecy was fulfilled in 1325. On the islands of Lake Texcoco, amid viper-infested marshes, the Aztecs built a city that they named Tenochtitlán in honor of Tenoch, who had guided them.

A few centuries later, another ethnic group, the Toltecs, founded the city of Tula, southwest of modern-day Mexico City. There they developed a brilliant civilization, raising their technical knowledge and arts to a high level, as attested by the finesse of their mosaics, paintings, sculptures, and sumptuous palaces. Ceremonies and cults in honor of their gods—including Quetzalcóatl—punctuated the life of the city and aimed to maintain the link with the cosmos and ensure the return of the rains and the growth of corn. But as the foundations of their society began to erode in the twelfth century, the Toltecs migrated and dispersed. In waves they founded new cities throughout the Great Valley, as far as the Yucatán Peninsula.

In the thirteenth century, a tribe from a mysterious city called Aztlán that worshiped, among other divinities, the god Tenoch set off on a journey. The god of war, Huitzilopochtli, prophesied that the tribe would settle when one of its members would see an eagle devouring a snake, perched atop a cactus. The famous prophecy was fulfilled in 1325. On the islands of Lake Texcoco, amid viper-infested marshes, the Aztecs built a city that they named Tenochtitlán in honor of Tenoch, who had guided them. In 1375, Acamapichtli became the first ruler and formed an alliance with the cities of Texcoco and Tlacopan. The triple alliance soon established its power over the region and triumphed over the Tepanecs in 1428.

Moctezuma I ascended the throne in 1440 and launched the "flower wars," with the aim of conquering new territories, imposing a tax on defeated peoples, and capturing enemies to offer them as sacrifices to the gods and appease their anger. Under his reign the empire expanded considerably. Moctezuma II, who succeeded him in 1502,

The Aztecs were remarkable builders and talented artists. They also developed a pictographic and ideographic writing system and transcribed their history and the stories of their gods in manuscripts known as codices.

continued his work. The city of Mexico-Tenochtitlán, supplied with water by an ingenious network of aqueducts and comprising natural and artificial islands on which sumptuous palaces, imposing temples, and splendid gardens had been built, was densely populated before the Spaniards arrived. It had a population of almost 200,000 and was home to a number of popular markets where goods from all over the empire were traded.

Aztec society was highly hierarchical, with the emperor, the members of the royal bloodline, the priests, and the lords at the top, followed by craftsmen, merchants, and the common people, and finally the slaves. The Aztecs were remarkable builders and talented artists. They also developed a pictographic and ideographic writing system and transcribed their history and the stories of their gods in manuscripts known as codices. They also devised an extremely elaborate calendar. The Aztecs were convinced that their gods had originally sacrificed themselves to create the sun, and that only massive human sacrifices could prevent the return of the Darkness. As the sun's chosen people, they engaged in this practice for years, performing regular ritual ceremonies that could last for several days, at the summit of the great temple. The Aztec calendar consisted of cycles that ended with the passing of one world and the beginning of a new one. To the great misfortune of the Aztecs and their neighbors, the return to Earth of the god Quetzalcóatl coincided with the year 1519 in the Gregorian calendar. It was precisely this coincidence that precipitated the fall of the Aztec Empire. Hernán Cortés, having rallied to his cause people who were tired of Aztec rule, entered Tenochtitlán, fully armored on his horse, parading before a people who had never seen horses and who believed that horse and rider were one and the same. Moctezuma and the dignitaries of the empire received him with honors befitting a god. Cortés and his lieutenants were showered with gold. Eager to receive even more gold, the Spaniards lost their senses and became brutal and cruel. The Aztecs, guessing that it was not the gods who had returned, rebelled against them and stoned Moctezuma, who had encouraged their misdeeds. On the night of June 30, 1520, known as la Noche Triste (the Night of Sorrows), the Aztecs drove the invaders out of Tenochtitlán at the instigation of the new emperor, Cuauhtémoc. This triumph was short lived.

Drawing on the support of peoples eager to bring down the Aztec Empire, Cortés attacked Tenochtitlán, and the city eventually surrendered on August 13, 1521. The Spaniards captured the emperor, crushed the troops, and conquered the city. They then proceeded to forcibly convert the Aztecs to Christianity and systematically destroy their culture by executing the members of the royal family, the lords, and the priests, smashing the statues of their gods and burning their codices. Speaking out against the cruelty of Cortés and his followers, the Dominican missionary Bartolomé de Las Casas vigorously denounced their crimes in his account *A Short Account of the Destruction of the Indies*. A few of his peers, including Bernardino de Sahagún, managed to snatch the codices from the flames and, in a hurry, recorded everything they could about the origins, customs, language, and beliefs of this civilization, which they had realized was on the verge of extinction. It is thanks to their efforts and foresight that the codices tell us and show us today what Aztec civilization was like at its height.

Eager to receive even more gold, the Spaniards lost their senses and became brutal and cruel. The Aztecs, guessing that it was not the gods who had returned, rebelled against them and stoned Moctezuma, who had encouraged their misdeeds.

THE INCAS

Sons of the sun god

Like the Olmecs, Mayans, and Aztecs, the Incas have fascinated generations of archeologists, historians, ethnologists, and adventurers with their customs, their worship of the sun god, and their remarkable pottery, jewelry, and textiles. While the causes of their tragic end are well known, the origins of the Incas remain shrouded in mystery. The Inca civilization, the last great empire of pre-Columbian America, was born and flourished in the heart of the Andes. Surprisingly, although it covered several thousand miles from central Chile to what is now Ecuador in its heyday, thanks in particular to a network of roads and a system of bridges suspended over vertiginous precipices, its glory days did not last more than a century.

The earliest origins of the Inca people date to 1800 BCE, to a group of farming and fishing communities on the coastal plains of Peru. The Chavin community, which flourished between 850 and 200 BCE, developed an art form that spread to central and southern Peru featuring half-animal, half-hu-

While the causes of their tragic end are well known, the origins of the Incas remain shrouded in mystery.

man divinities. In 100 BCE, the Moche and their splendid artistic creations laid the foundations for a civilization that was to rule the region brilliantly and cruelly for more than eight centuries. Their hegemony was crushed by the Huaris, who also defeated their Nazca neighbors and kept the Tiwanaku, whose empire was in full expansion, in check. Around the year 1000, the empires of the Huaris and the Tiwanaku imploded and a number of microstates emerged. The Incas, warriors and hunters who made their home in the plateau region south of Peru's central cordillera, were one of them.

According to several legends, Manco Cápac, son of the sun god, created the Quechua people who gave birth to the Incas—the "children of the sun." At the end of the twelfth century, he led them from their caves to a fertile valley, where they founded Cuzco. For two centuries the Incas lived in peace with their neighbors. At the beginning of the fifteenth century, under the reign of Viracocha, they began to harbor hopes of conquest. Under the reigns of the emperor Cusi Yupanqui, known as Pachacutec (1438–71), and his successor, Túpac Yupanqui (1471–93), they defeated their neighbors and assimilated them. The wealth they acquired enabled them to build sumptuous palaces and temples in Cuzco.

Once in power, Huayna Capac (1493–1527) subdued several more peoples. By the fourteenth century he was at the head of a powerful empire. Ta-

huantinsuyu, as it was called by its subjects, which meant "Realm of the Four Parts" in Quechua, was home to ten million inhabitants and stretched more than 3,100 miles along the Andes. The empire was highly hierarchical and disciplined. By strictly dividing labor, the empire enjoyed remarkable prosperity from an intensive farming of potatoes and corn and rearing of alpacas, whose soft wool was greatly appreciated.

> *The Sapa Inca ruled from the empire's capital, Cuzco (Quechua for "navel of the earth"), where they made sure that laws were firmly enforced. This is also where the emperor built his sumptuous palace and the Temple of the Sun.*

The supreme god, creator of life and death, of all beings and all things was Viracocha. But the Incas also worshiped the gods of the moon, the stars, time, the earth, the harvest . . . Of all the cults, the most spectacular were those paid to the sun god. His representative on Earth was the Sapa Inca, the emperor himself, and honoring the sun god meant honoring the emperor by covering the temples in gold.

The Sapa Inca ruled from the empire's capital, Cuzco (Quechua for "navel of the earth"), where they made sure that laws were firmly enforced. This is also where the emperor built his sumptuous palace and the Temple of the Sun. The Incas were great builders who constructed their homes in stone so that they would not be swept away by earthquakes. They also designed a gigantic network of paved roads stretching for thousands of miles and built suspension bridges for messengers on foot to carry the orders of the Sapa Inca throughout the empire. In 1527, the death of Huayna Capac plunged the empire into a violent dynastic feud. Both Huáscar and Atahualpa claimed the throne and waged a bloody war, dragging their people into the process. Atahualpa eventually won in 1532, but the empire had suffered greatly from their fratricidal conflict. Weakened and divided, it was not prepared to face the danger that awaited. To the Incas' great misfortune, 1532 also marked the beginning of their collapse. That year, Francisco Pizarro and his 180 men landed on the Peruvian coast. With his full beard, his helmet, his armor, and his horse, the Spanish conquistador was, just as Hernán Cortés had been when he entered Aztec lands, mistaken for a god making his grand return. On November 16, 1532, during a meeting between an expedition he had led and an Inca delegation that had come to meet him, Francisco Pizarro treacherously cap-

*The conquistadores enslaved
the Incas, converted them to
Christianity, plundered their
temples, and destroyed them.*

tured Atahualpa. With the emperor at the mercy of the invaders, the petrified Incas, still weakened by their divisions, were unable to fight back, and it was without encountering the slightest resistance that the Spaniards took Cuzco. After receiving incredible quantities of silver and gold from all over the empire, Pizarro had Atahualpa executed. Under the authority of a new emperor, Manco Capac II, a timid resistance began to organize itself in the mountains. However, the defeats his proud warriors suffered in the face of the superiority of the Spaniards, and the diseases brought over from Europe, decimated them within a few years. Without mercy, the conquistadores enslaved the Incas, converted them to Christianity, plundered their temples, and destroyed them. In 1572, Túpac Amaru I, the last Inca emperor, was captured and executed by the Spanish. His passing marked the end of the last "Son of the Sun" and of the most-thriving civilizations in Mesoamerica.

Thanks to the Quechua language and the *quipus*, Inca culture did not disappear entirely. In 1911, American archeologist Hiram Bingham went on a quest to find the last emperor's hidden lair. He followed his guides to a place high in the mountains. With a lot of patience and hard work, Hiram Bingham and his team achieved the impossible: they succeeded in unearthing the ruins of the sacred city from the mountains. Their efforts had paid off. In June 1912 he wrote in his notebooks, as he contemplated the fruit of their labors, "*Here the clearing has worked wonders: the intihuatana and the terraces to the west of the sacred square are finally emerging from the forest. The vertiginous precipices are appearing to the left and, far below, the bubbling, rumbling Urubamba River. . . . The Sacred City was well and truly an impenetrable place!*" Hiram Bingham and his team had succeeded; they had uncovered the exceptional site of Machu Picchu, the final resting place of the Inca Sapa, high up in the mountains to escape the fury of the barbarians.

THE ANASAZI

....

Builders of cave cities

....

The origins of the Anasazi Indians, the "Ancient Ones" in the Navajo language, who thrived on the plateaus of the so-called Four Corners region, on the borders of present-day states Colorado, Utah, Arizona, and New Mexico, remain just as much a mystery as many aspects of their history.

In the first centuries CE, the Anasazi—the main group of Pueblo Indians—began to settle on the Mesa Verde site. From 450 to 700 CE, they lived by growing corn and squash and hunting and gathering. They made objects from woven rope and ceramics and built pit houses with central hearths and wooden roof supports. They founded their first villages at the foot of rocky outcrops, before settling on plateaus known as mesas. From the eighth century onward they built villages with rectangular, stone-walled houses and began to paint ritual dances and ceremonies on rocks. In the next century, following extraordinary population growth, they built structures in clay and mud bricks. One of the most important buildings, which housed crop reserves and comprised more than two hundred rooms, including some twenty kivas (circular, sometimes monumental, underground structures used as dwellings, as well as places of worship and ceremony), was called the Cliff Palace. On the Mesa Verde site, the Anasazi began building large architectural complexes in gigantic rockshelters that they dug right into the

canyon wall; four thousand sites, including several hundred troglodytic dwellings, were discovered. By the middle of the thirteenth century, 20,000 people were living there. This made for a sizable population. In fact, given that the main crop they cultivated was corn and that game and drinking-water sources were scarce, the population was probably too large.

In 1921, at Chaco Canyon in New Mexico, archeologists noticed three massive sandstone blocks on a high knoll that were arranged in such a way that they allowed the sun's rays to penetrate through two slits and illuminate two spirals engraved on the mountain rock. For a long time, this unusual structure was a source of wonder. What did these spirals represent? What was their function? Archeologists discovered that they were calendars on which the sun's rays marked the summer and winter solstices, as well as the equinoxes of March and September. Strange pictograms were also found on ocher rocks and confirmed the Anasazi's extensive knowledge of astronomy, which was quite remarkable for its time. After studying a series of pictograms, archeologists hypothesized that this civilization witnessed the appearance of a star born from the explosion of a supernova, a spectacular phenomenon that would have occurred in the middle of the tenth century, on the night of July 5, 1054. The crescent waning moon (in an inverted position) was 2 degrees from the Crab Nebula. It was this motif of an inverted crescent moon that archeologists discovered painted or engraved in various parts of Chaco Canyon. Could this cataclysm have been the source of their burning desire to understand the mysteries of the heavens?

The Anasazi Indians mapped out and designed a network of 500 miles of perfectly straight, 32-foot-wide roads. Many of these roads ran from Chaco Canyon to the villages, but others ended nowhere, stopping in the middle of the desert, under the immense sky of New Mexico. Did they exist to communicate with some invisible world? For a long time the network of roads, the culture, and its symbols fueled the wildest hypotheses and assertions, especially given that the Anasazi disappeared and abandoned their troglodytic homes at the beginning of the thirteenth century. What were the causes of this sudden departure?

The demise of the Anasazi was caused by a combination of factors: drought and a rapidly growing population led to a depletion of resources, which in turn led to armed conflict. While the Anasazi migrated in droves in search of new territories and resources, it seems that the most-desperate individuals, refusing to leave the lands of their ancestors, ended up tearing each other apart and resorting to cannibalism to avoid starvation.

To this day, what remains of this nation of builders who sought to understand the mysteries of the galaxy? Paths traced for hundreds of miles, pottery

It was said that, convinced of their multidimensional existence, the Anasazi practiced rituals enabling them to travel through time.

left over from their artistic production, and pictograms engraved on rocks, which, like the roads leading into barren lands, have not yet revealed all their secrets. They will no doubt remain enigmas for a long time to come. It was said that, convinced of their multidimensional existence, the Anasazi practiced rituals enabling them to travel through time. The spirals engraved on the cave walls are said to represent the galaxy, symbolizing the link between them and beings from elsewhere . . . Other petroglyphs refer to the ant people, cosmic travelers who appeared on Earth to help found humanity, and who enabled the Anasazi to survive a cataclysm by taking them underground. Are these made-up tales? Strangely enough, the Hopi tribe share the same myth.

THE MANDINKA

The prosperous kingdom of Mali

Of all the empires on the Dark Continent, the Mali Empire in the Manding region of Africa was the largest. And yet, in the seventh century, the Mandinka kingdom, in the region of Manding (or Manden), in the upper Niger, was no more than a modest chiefdom. Its center was the present-day town of Kangaba, whose inhabitants were known as the Mandinka or Malinke. For three centuries, they led an unremarkable existence under the authority of their rulers from the Keita clan. The kingdom's destiny changed in the eleventh century.

Mali's remarkable development benefited from crafts, the slave trade, ivory, salt, and gold, exploiting the deposits scattered throughout its territory.

In 1050, the Mandingo ruler Baramendena traveled to Mecca to make his pilgrimage and was converted to Islam by a member of the Almoravid dynasty. On his return, he freed himself from the authority of the empire of Ghana and established relations with his neighbors, who encouraged the growth of his kingdom. Baramendena exploited the gold mines of Bouré, which gradually eclipsed those of Bambouk. This overturned the balance of power among Ghana, Sudan, and North Africa. Taking advantage of the disintegration of Ghana and the fact that its territory was at the crossroads of the nomadic routes of the Sahara and the populations of the equatorial regions, Mali based its remarkable growth on crafts, the slave trade, ivory, salt, and gold, exploiting the deposits scattered across its territory. At the same time, the lands of the Niger loop, more fertile than ever, encouraged the development of agriculture and contributed greatly to the kingdom's prosperity. The meteoric rise of the ruler of the modest chieftaincy of Kangaba and the rapid enrichment of the kingdom of Mali soon aroused covetousness. Soumaoro Kanté, king of the Sosso people, was the first to try to get his hands on the rich resources of the prosperous neighboring kingdom. In 1224, after subduing the chiefdoms and tiny kingdoms and building up an army, he conquered and annexed Manding to his kingdom.

Sundiata Keita, who was to become the hero of the Mandingo Empire and whose deeds would be sung by griots (West African storytellers) in a formidable epic, was the grandson of Baramendena's successor. It was he who federated and united under his banner the chiefs of the Manding territories surrounding Kangaba and formed an army of 10,000 cavalry and 100,000 infantry soldiers. He led his army to fight against Soumangourou Kanté, whom he defeated at Kirina in 1235.

The year 1307 marked the beginning of the reign of Mansa Musa. Under his rule the Mandinka Empire reached the height of its power. Mansa Musa was a conqueror who extended the borders of the empire and built mosques across all the countries in the name of Islam.

Legend has it that Soumangomou Kanté disappeared in the mountains near the town of Koulikoro. With the strength of his army and the element of surprise, Soundiata captured the enemies' city of Sosso, then Koumbi Saleh, the stronghold of the empire of Ghana, which had once proudly ruled Africa, and he established his capital in Niani. He died in 1255. According to legend, he drowned in the Sankarani River and was reborn as a hippopotamus. The man known to his people as the "king of kings" left behind a prosperous kingdom where the various ethnic groups lived together peacefully. His successors,

Oulé and then Sakura, considerably extended the borders to the west and north and forged trade links with new partners, gloriously continuing the work begun by Sundiata.

The year 1307 marked the beginning of the reign of Mansa Musa. Under his rule the Mandinka Empire reached the height of its power. Mansa Musa was a conqueror who extended the empire's borders to Djenné, Gao, and Timbuktu. In Gao, Mansa Musa ordered the architect Abu Ishaq al-Sahili to build a decent mosque in place of the miserable shack that served as a place of prayer. Es-Sahéli complied, building a brick edifice with crenellated walls and a pyramidal minaret: the Djingareyber Mosque. He built an identical mosque in Timbuktu, and other mosques were built throughout the country on the same model. When Mansa Musa died in 1337, the empire was at its peak. The year after his death, the Mossi people seized Timbuktu and sacked it: this was the empire's first serious blow. Mansa Musa's successors were unable to stop the repeated attacks on their possessions by the Tuaregs, the Mossi people, and the Songhai. And so began the fragmentation of the Mali Empire. In 1430, Timbuktu fell to the Tuareg, and the splendor of the Mandinka people reached its conclusion.

On the basis of the accounts of Arab-Berber informants, the Portuguese chronicler Gomes Eanes de Zurara reported in his *Chronicle of Discovery and Conquest of Guinea* in 1453 on the contacts made by his compatriots with the inhabitants of the "Kingdom of Melli," in the Manding region. For the Portuguese, the Manding region was vaguely perceived as a "great kingdom," which they just as vaguely located in what they then called the "land of the Blacks."

For half a century, the information provided by geographers and chroniclers was confusing. It was not until 1506 that real insights into the Mali Empire were provided in the Valentim Fernandes manuscript:

"In this Ethiopia, from Cabo Verde to the Casamance River, they are all circumcised, and the majority belong to the cult of Mohammed. And the two greatest generations of Ethyopes are Gylafo and Mandinka. These have in common a great king, who they call Mandimansa. . . . This king is lord of many who pay him many tributes. He lives more than four hundred leagues inland, in a city surrounded by adobe." By the time Valentim Fernandes published his manuscript *Descripcam*, this knowledge had been obsolete for several decades. So as not to let the empire's greatness wither away, Mandinka storytellers in the villages of West Africa passed on, from generation to generation, the story of Sundiata, which they recount to the sounds of the xalam, the traditional West African lute. Even today, storytellers continue to tell the story of Sundiata, the Mandinka Epic. *"I sing, I call for Sundiata / Son of Sogolon, the female buffalo / The son of Konaté, of the Keita lion dynasty / I call the founder of the Mali Empire / I sing the praises of he who united ten kingdoms / From deep in Sudan to the ocean / Home to people speaking ten languages / Who never stopped fighting each other / I remember the story of the brave warrior / Who knew how to fight, conquer and pacify / Africa's largest empire."* (extract from *Sundiata: The Lion Child* by Lilyan Kesteloot).

So as not to let the empire's greatness wither away, Mandinka storytellers in the villages of West Africa passed on, from generation to generation, the story of Sundiata, the Mandinka Epic.

TASMANIAN ABORIGINAL PEOPLE

....

From horror to abomination

....

A slow, tremendous rise in sea level turned the northern tip of present-day Australia into an island. Despite being cut off from the mainland, the island's inhabitants, who had been living on this peninsula for almost 40,000 years, did not remain isolated and began to trade with fishers from neighboring archipelagos.

On his search of the famous southern continent, Dutch navigator Abel Tasman was arguably the first European to discover the island, in 1642. Although he did not stop here, he named it Diemensland (Van Diemen's Land) in honor of Anthony Van Diemen, governor of the Dutch East Indies, who had generously financed his expedition. For more than two centuries the island was only occasionally visited by Europeans, who, with the exception of a few observers, described all its inhabitants—then simply called "the blacks of this country"—as some of the rudest savages they had encountered until then. Between 1773 and 1792,

Tobias Furneaux, James Cook, and James Bligh stopped on the island. When Nicolas Baudin's expedition landed there in 1802, three scientists spent time with the Aboriginal women, gathering valuable information on the customs, technical knowledge, and beliefs of their people.

In 1803, the English Crown seized the island to create a colony on the banks of the Derwent River. The following year, the modest colony moved to the site where the town of Hobart now stands. Between five thousand and seven thousand Aboriginal people lived in these hunting-and-gathering lands. Although relations between the two communities were peaceful at first, the British soon came to regard the customs, techniques, and beliefs of the locals as frustratingly crude and inferior to those of their neighbors in Australia, and they used their superiority to take over the lands of the Aborigines and drive them out. Less than three-quarters of a century passed before the last member of the Tasmanian Aboriginal people died out.

For the first ten years the British and the Tasmanians fought fiercely, since the English Crown chose the island as the final destination for its unwanted citizens. Convicts poured in by the boatload and rapidly outnumbered the settlers. At first the Tasmanians died in the hundreds, decimated by the fighting and the diseases that had been introduced by the settlers. Hundreds more died during the Black War between 1825 and 1831,

In 1802, three scientists spent time with Aboriginal women and gathered valuable information on the customs, technical knowledge, and beliefs of their people.

which opposed them to the British. From 1829 to 1834, the locals were deported to Flinders Island. Those who did not die were transferred to Oyster Cove, while those who hid to escape deportation were hunted like wild animals. Grim details: rewards of 5 pounds and 2 pounds were given to anyone who captured adults and children, respectively. By 1847, only a few dozen Tasmanian Aboriginal people were left to languish in Oyster Cove. Photographs of the last Tasmanian Aboriginal people date from this period. The last of what the British Empire considered to be its scum population was transported to the island in 1853. Van Diemen's Land was renamed Tasmania in honor of the man who discovered it, and was now home to 74,000 convicts. This was the final chapter in the extinc-

Although relations between the two communities were peaceful at first, the British soon came to regard the customs, techniques, and beliefs of the locals as frustratingly crude and inferior to those of their neighbors in Australia.

tion of the land's original inhabitants. Truganini's tragic destiny represents the terrible and painful embodiment of this history. Born on Bruny Island in 1812, Truganini suffered many personal tragedies. She resisted oppression before working with her husband, Woorrady, and George Robinson, the Protector of Aborigines, to save the last representatives of her people when they were moved to the Flinders Island reserve. With the help of four companions, she escaped and went into hiding, but Truganini was recaptured. Injured during her capture and treated at Bass River, she was imprisoned for several months before being returned to Flinders Island. She was then transported with the last survivors of her people to Oyster Cove in 1856. Five years later, the Colonial Office revealed that there were only fourteen Tasmanian Aboriginal people still alive—nine women and five men. None of the four couples had children. Reduced to idle, alcoholic drifters, Truganini and her people lived the rest of their lives in Oyster Cove, where they died one by one.

In Jules Verne's novel *In Search of the Castaways*, published in 1868, the main protagonists crisscrossed Australia, and the author did not fail to mention the abuses committed by the British as part of what the perfidious British henchmen claimed to be the virtuous spread of civilization. The narrator wrote, "*The English, at the beginning of their conquest, employed murder as an aid to col-*

onization. Their cruel atrocities were numerous. They behaved in Australia as they had in India, where five million Indians have disappeared, and as they did in the Cape, where a population of one million Hottentots fell to a hundred thousand. The Aboriginal population, decimated by mistreatment and drunkenness, is gradually disappearing from the continent before a homicidal civilization. Some governors, it is true, have issued decrees against the bloodthirsty bushmen. A few white men who cut off a Black man's nose and ears, or his little finger 'to make a pipe cleaner,' were punished with a few lashes. This was a vain threat. Murder was organized on a vast scale, and whole tribes disappeared. In Tasmania alone, which had fifteen thousand natives at the beginning of the century, the native population was reduced to seven by 1863; and recently the Mercury announced the arrival of the last of the Tasmanians at Hobart." This was Truganini. She was brought to Hobart in 1873 as the last remaining survivor of her people, and three years later she passed away, alone and sad after a life of suffering and death.

At the time, the bodies of the natives were cut up and dissected like those of animals. On her deathbed, Truganini pleaded with her doctor not to suffer this fate. She pleaded for her ashes to be scattered in the D'Entrecasteaux Channel, opposite her native island. At first her request was granted, and her body was not mutilated. But after horror comes abomination, and her body was

"The Aboriginal population, decimated by mistreatment and drunkenness, is gradually disappearing from the continent before a homicidal civilization."

finally exhumed, with her skeleton displayed in a showcase at the Tasmanian Museum. It remained there until 1947, when it was finally removed after numerous complaints. In 1976, to mark the centenary of Truganini's death, her skeleton was cremated and the ashes thrown into the sea in accordance with her wishes.

In 2002, in the hope to making amends for one of the darkest chapters in the history of British colonization, the Royal College of Surgeons of England presented a Tasmanian delegation with the remains of Truganini's skin and hair, as well as the bones of other Aborigines, so that they could be buried on their native land.

THE NIVKH

Ghosts of Sakhalin Island

Who were the Nivkh (or Gilyak, as they were known to the Russians) that Chekhov and, one hundred years later, Haruki Murakami wrote about? Their origins go back a long way. During the early Quaternary period, people who called themselves the Nivkh lived on today's Sakhalin Island, which back then was attached to the mainland. At the end of the ice age, as the waters rose, their population was split in two. Isolated on an inhospitable island, the Nivkh of Sakhalin lived removed from the rest of the globe for several centuries. Their contacts with the mainland were limited to exchanges with their relatives. During the Yuan dynasty, Chinese chronicles from the twelfth century mention relations between the mainland Nivkh, called Gilyami by the Chinese, who were under the guardianship of the Manchu Empire.

It was not until the seventeenth century that Russian travelers recognized the Asian frontier and came into contact with these people. The explorer **Vasily Poiarkov**, who encountered them in the 1640s, named them Gilyak. For two centuries, Russian peasants settled on their lands and in their proximity until the Russian Empire claimed the lands for itself in 1856, following the signing of the Treaty of Aigun. At the same time, the Treaty of Shimoda divided Sakhalin Island between the **Russian Empire** and Japanese Tokugawa shogunate. The land was partitioned along the fiftieth parallel. The following year the Russians opened a forced-labor camp. Thieves, murderers, and exiles were deported en masse and died there under the watchful eye of the Gilyak, who had been displaced from their traditional way of life by the Czarist Empire.

The Gilyak, who were used to the harsh climate and environment, had lived for centuries by gathering, hunting, and fishing. The shamans watched over the community, governing a spiritual life in which they considered many animal species to be their equals. Bears were perceived by the Gilyak as the incarnation of ancestors and divinities and were celebrated. Every year, a bear that had been raised in the community for many years was celebrated with great festivities that culminated in its sacrifice.

The Gulyak's simple way of life in harmony with nature was affected both by Russian domination and Japanese rule, with each power using different but equally violent methods. Anton Chekhov, who went there to report on the labor camp, met the Gulyak, whose strange customs were talked about. His travel notes from his time on Sakhalin Island painted a poignant portrait of these proud people whose manners suggested that they had once been a great nation. The Gulyak were decimated by epidemics of smallpox, plague, and chronic influenza and suffered from displacement and relocation. And although they have not entirely disappeared, they are still fighting to preserve what remains of their culture, customs, and dialects.

THE INDIANS OF NORTH AMERICA

"Damned savages"

"*God created this Indian country and it was like He spread out a big blanket. He put the Indians on it.*" The blanket was the North American continent, and the earliest human presence on this land is thought to date to 60,000 years BP. These humans came from Asia through the Bering Strait during the ice ages and gradually scattered across America. The last to settle here were the Inuit, in the northernmost reaches of the continent.

According to archeological evidence, the first contact between Europeans and Native Americans occurred in the tenth century, between Vikings and the natives on the northeastern coast of present-day Newfoundland.

Of all the peoples who settled this vast land over the centuries, many, such as the Hohokam and Mogollon, died out before the arrival of Europeans. According to archeological evidence, the first contact between Native Americans and Europeans occurred in the tenth century, between the Vikings and the natives of the northeastern coast, in what is now the province of Newfoundland, where the Northmen set up camp. Could the land they set up camp on be the Vinland described in the Norse sagas? Could the Indians be the famous *skraelings*? Undoubtedly. However, because of constant disputes the Vikings did not stay long. For decades the Portuguese, Normans, and English came to fish cod in these waters.

At the beginning of the sixteenth century, Jean Cabot, Jacques Cartier, Giovanni da Verrazzano, and Juan Fernández made several trips up rivers and estuaries, exploring coasts, bays, and lands. They established contact with tribes and founded trading posts for furs—particularly beaver and otter, which were highly prized—over the course of the century. The English started doing the same in the center, and the Spanish in Florida to the south. Violence, kidnapping, rape, and murder put an end to this entente, and the natives retreated into the forests. The arrival of the Pilgrim fathers and their Puritan families aboard the *Mayflower* and the founding of the thirteen New England colonies marked a decisive turning point in the relations between the Native Americans—the Narragansett and the Wampanoag tribes notably—and the Europeans. The Puritans may have immediately regarded the natives as "sons of Satan," but they would not have survived the frigid winters if it had not been for their help. Several confederations of Indian tribes governed the continent from north to south: the Algonquin peoples ruled the North.

The Chippewa, Cree, Miami, Delaware, Shawnee, Ottawa, Arapaho, Blackfoot, Cheyenne, and the procession of Iroquois Indians, to mention only the best-known tribes, clans, and nations, lived around and above the Great Lakes. The Sioux, Wichita, and Comanche lived peacefully in the vast lands of the South.

In the second half of the eighteenth century, the Iroquois, who were the English's proxies against the French, who were in alliance with the Algonquin and Wyandot people, thought they could use their new friends to eliminate their sworn enemies. Irrespective of the alliances that were formed, the outcome was the same for all. At the end of the eighteenth century, Shawnee chief Tecumseh addressed his people, appealing to the memory of vanished tribes: "*Where today are the Pequot? Where are the Narragansett, the Mohican, the Pokanoket, and many other once-powerful tribes of our people? They have vanished before the avarice and oppression of the white man, as snow before the summer sun.*" The birth of the American nation led the American Indians to believe for a time that the intentions of the Americans would be different from those of the British. They soon realized that the white man, whatever his flag, was interested only in land. One by one, American Indian nations and confederations were forced to surrender all or part of their territories. The American Indian alliances were swept away by American troops in a few decisive battles, such as the Battle of Fallen Timbers in 1794. Tecumseh was probably the last great chief to attempt to unite the Indian nations: "*The annihilation of our race is at hand unless we unite in one common cause against the common foe.*" But it was too late. To escape the

In the space of half a century, the settlers' desire to expand and evangelize the "savages" precipitated the fate and destruction of the Native American nations. More deadly than the wars, their unhappy alliances with the English or French, the wars between tribes, or their enslavement, it was epidemics—diseases such as whooping cough, influenza, measles, cholera, and smallpox—that the Europeans had brought over with them that decimated the natives in droves.

ambitions of settlers and newcomers, many Native American peoples migrated inland, leading a peaceful seminomadic existence and hunting buffalo. In the mid-nineteenth century, settlers set out to conquer the West, pushing back even farther the tribes already driven out, laying railroad tracks and telegraph wires to link east and west and eradicating villages.

By slaughtering the buffalo, the settlers dealt a fatal blow to the Native Americans' fragile ecological balance. To halt the progress of these newcomers, which was as meteoric as it was destructive, the Sioux tribes forged alliances with the Arapaho and Cheyenne. This was the start of the American Indian Wars, which saw the rise of great chiefs who would become legends: the Sioux leaders Sitting Bull and Crazy Horse.

In this merciless war the Native Americans fought back, relentlessly attacking pioneer convoys, farms, and forts. They proved to be as determined and cruel as the settlers. They won several major battles, including the Battle of the Little Bighorn in 1876. The uproar caused by this defeat convinced the settlers it was time to deal the final blow. They continued to hunt down and fight the natives until the Wounded Knee Massacre in 1890, which significantly quashed the resistance. Treaties were signed, imposing a white peace, and the natives were herded into reservations. From a population of 850,000 when Columbus first arrived on the continent, only 50,000 remained.

Assimilated, acculturated, and reduced to being dependent on government benefits and assistance, many Native Americans plunged into violence and alcoholism. Throughout the twentieth century, descendants of those who were "the first Americans" relentlessly promoted their culture, denounced the atrocities and massacres to which their ancestors were subjected, and promoted their spiritual heritage in an effort to contain the collapse of their community. Today their children are carrying on this fight.

Assimilated, acculturated, and reduced to being dependent on government benefits and assistance, many Native Americans plunged into violence and alcoholism.

THE SELK'NAM

The tragedy of the Salesian mission on Dawson Island

Among the tribes that populated the desolate islets of Tierra del Fuego, including the Yahgan, Chono, and Kawésqar, were the Selk'nam, also known as the Onawo, or Ona people. Were these the Indians whose fires Magellan spotted in 1520, when his ships slipped through the strait that later took his name? The Selk'nam were hunters and gatherers who lived in the northeast of Tierra del Fuego. They survived in this extremely hostile environment on a diet of shellfish, crustaceans, birds, and guanacos. For three centuries, ships flying Spanish, Dutch, and English flags anchored or wrecked in the area as they tried to search for the fabulous City of the Caesars. Their crews made contact with the Alakaluf, Chono, and Yahgan tribes. Although relations between foreigners and natives were generally peaceful, some ended in bloodshed. By the end of the eighteenth century, the Yahgan and Chono had died out. The Selk'nam, who were stronger and more numerous than their neighbors and constantly moved into unoccupied territories, were able to avoid aggression for a long time.

In the 1880s, the carving up of Tierra del Fuego indirectly caused the tragic disappearance of the Selk'nam.

In the 1880s, by carving up Tierra del Fuego, Chilean authorities, landowners, and ranchers indirectly caused the tragic disappearance of the Selk'nam. To take over the lands, the Chilean government relocated the Tehuelche people, who now numbered only a hundred or so, to a modest reserve. While the lands occupied by the Yahgan were not yet part of those the settlers planned to exploit, and those occupied by the Kawésqar were so desolate that they did not interest the Chilean authorities, the lands on which the Selk'nam had settled provided good grazing for sheep and became the object of much attention. How many Selk'nam were there at the time? Several thousand? According to the estimate of Swedish explorer Otto Nordenskjöld, they could have numbered 1,500. Or maybe a few hundred at most? Because these nomads were constantly on the move to maintain their way of life and escape the settlers, it was impossible to count them reliably. Despite the Selk'nam's relentless, exhausting wandering, the companies and first settlers—ruthless expeditionists and penniless adventurers drawn by the wealth of resources of these promised new lands—showed no mercy toward the Selk'nam. They killed off those who found themselves in the pastures they intended for their sheep, whose wool and flesh were surely more precious than people they considered to be miserable, bedraggled bums. Many conflicts broke out. Murdered, attacked, and dispossessed, the Selk'nam tried

to resist and fight back with their meager resources. Since they were always a presence rather
than a threat, the colonists easily eliminated the
factious ones. The growing number of incidents
between Selk'nam and settlers forced authorities to take action. After thinking for a while of
erecting a border and posts, they opted for a less
costly project concealed under the guise of good
intentions: the Selk'nam would be deported to a
mission to civilize them and teach them religion.
The mission was to be established on one of the
most ungrateful little islands of Tierra del Fuego:
Dawson Island. The Chilean government granted
this concession to the Salesian religious order. In
1890, the mission was equipped with a school, a
sawmill, and carpentry workshops and welcomed
first Kawésqar and then Selk'nam, most of whom
had been captured.

In 1896, dozens of ragged Selk'nam were driven
to join the mission to overcome famine and the
terrible harshness of winter. Despite the good-
will and pious wishes of the fathers, the Sale-
sians' work was a failure and a human tragedy.
Would deporting savages that were treated as
beasts and making them work wood really help
civilize them? The failure to teach them to read
and write, combined with the isolation of the mission, meant that the Selk'nam could never hope
to find a place in Chilean society. Additionally,
an unprecedented mortality rate inexplicably
struck down the Selk'nam children at the turn of
the century. As a result, the Selk'nam people died
out in the space of two decades, amid general in-
difference. By the time the gigantic graveyard of a
mission closed its doors in 1911, more than eight
hundred natives had died.

Murdered, attacked, and dis-possessed, the Selk'nam tried to resist and fight back with their meager resources.

In 1953, the ethnologist José Emperaire wrote:
*"Nobody will ever know how many Selk'nam were
murdered. The interests and individuals still at
stake continue to create a wall of silence around this
50-year-old affair to protect fortunes. Whether it was
a hundred or a thousand, the fact remains that many
Selk'nam were massacred, and irreparable monstros-
ities were committed when Tierra del Fuego was first
colonized."* To this day, we still do not know how
many Selk'nam were victim to this ethnocide.

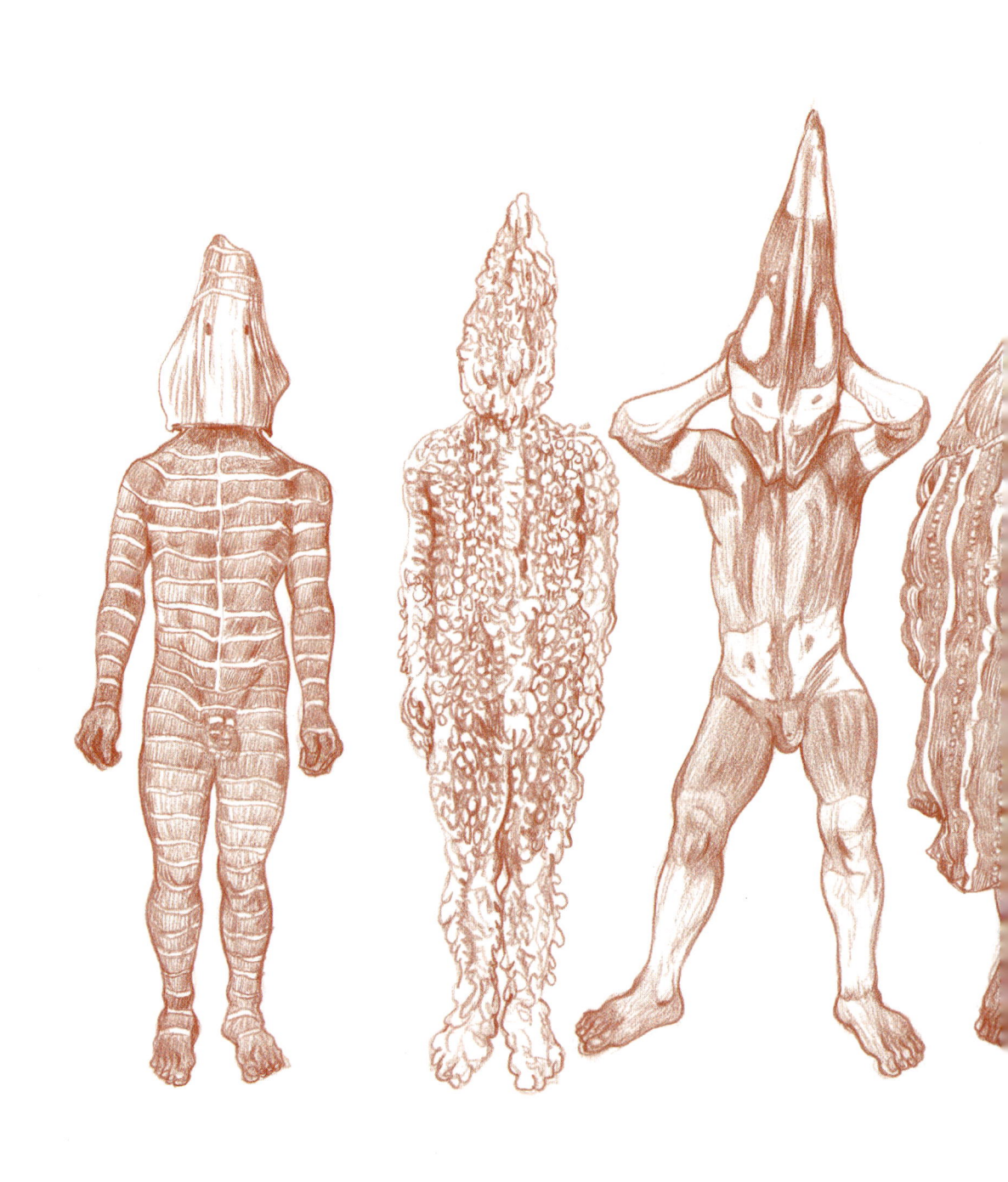

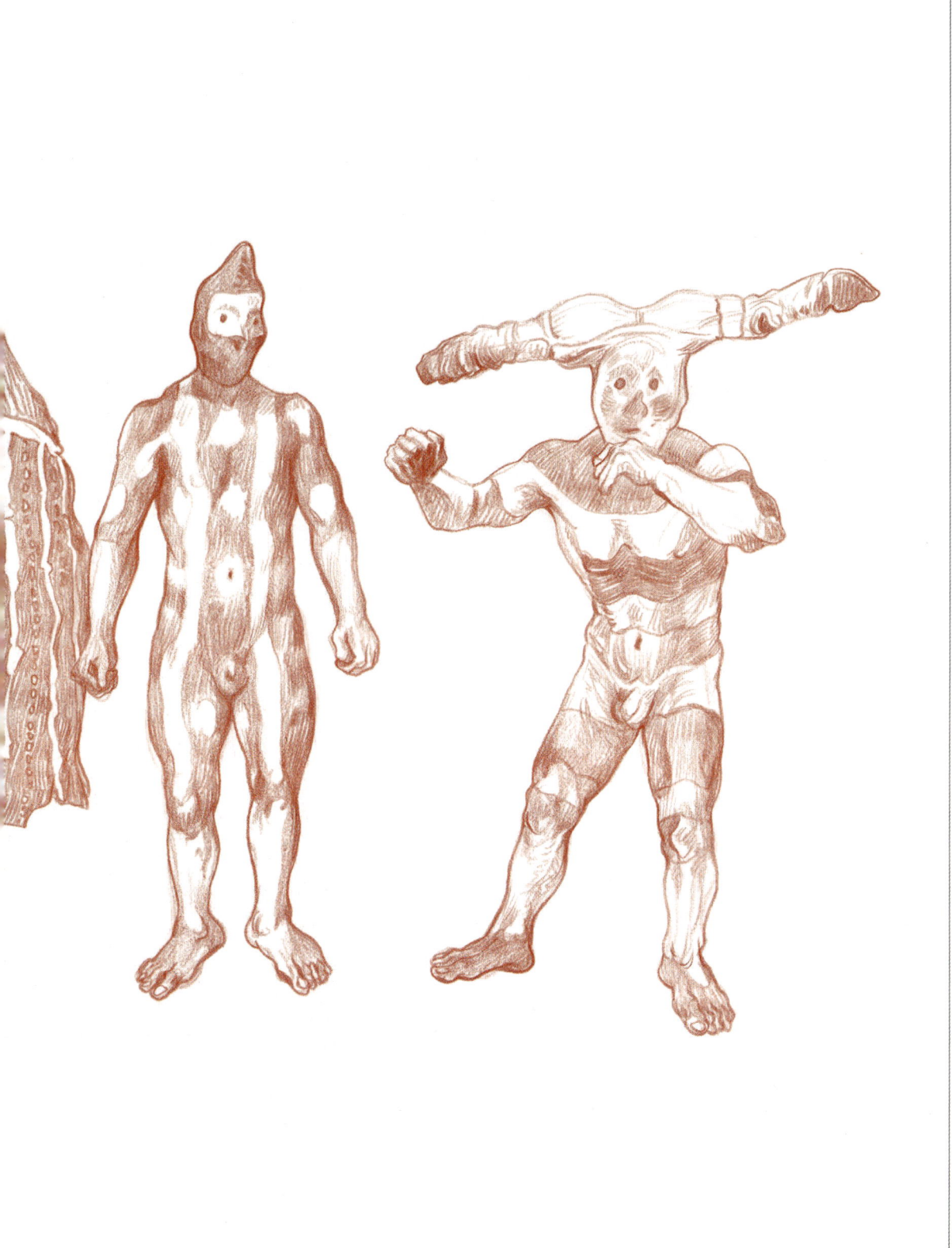

THE HERERO AND THE NAMA

An unfinished extermination

In the 1840s, members of the Evangelical Church in Germany's Rhineland region set out to establish missions in territories overlooked by colonizers in the southwestern tip of Africa, in present-day Namibia. The gigantic yet semidesertic and inhospitable territory was home to the Herero and Nama. Some Herero chiefs formed alliances with the colonizers in exchange for protection and material goods, others forged alliances with Afrikaners, and others still chose to keep their distance from white people.

In the early 1880s, German missionaries and merchants settled on the coast, and a merchant from Bremen acquired land from local chiefs. With the German Empire seriously lagging behind in the race for colonies, Bismarck did not want to miss the opportunity to seize such a vast territory, and so the German South-West African Protectorate was proclaimed on August 7, 1884. When the administration of the German Empire took possession of the colony, the Herero population numbered 80,000 and the Nama around 20,000. The German colony stagnated. With the arrival of the first German troops in 1889, incidents, attacks,

The settlers exploited the natives, robbed them of their livestock, and stole their women.

and massacres over land and cattle theft began to multiply between settlers and natives. By annexing the lands of the chiefs they defeated, and by multiplying treaties with chiefs with whom they had formed alliances, the German authorities were able to acquire vast territories, livestock, and workforce. The settlers exploited the natives on their plantations, robbed them of their livestock, and stole their women. By the turn of the century, the Herero and Nama had lost their independence.

In 1904, suffering from appalling living conditions, mistreatment, and abuse, the Herero rebelled and massacred more than a hundred settlers. Ethnic nationalism, based on the idea that blood is connected to the soil and the belief that human beings can be divided into several races, was popular in the German Empire at the time. Firmly resolved to transform this desolate but mineral-rich territory into a prosperous white settlement, the empire retaliated. The eradication of the Herero was underway.

Six months later, General Lothar von Trotha arrived in the colony with 3,500 soldiers. On August 11, 1904, his troops crushed the Herero rebellion, massacring more than five thousand fighters during the Battle of Waterberg and driving off tens of thousands of civilians who had joined the rebellion. The survivors fled into the Kalahari Desert, where the Germans had poisoned the main wells and pursued them for weeks. On October 2,

Trotha issued the following extermination order: "*I, the great general of the German soldiers, send this letter to the Hereros. The Hereros are German subjects no longer. They have killed, stolen, cut off the ears and other parts of the body of wounded soldiers, and now are too cowardly to want to fight any longer. I announce to the people that whoever hands me one of the chiefs shall receive 1,000 marks, and 5,000 marks for Samuel Maherero. The Herero nation must now leave the country. If it refuses, I shall compel it to do so with the 'long tube' (cannon). Any Herero found inside the German frontier, with or without a gun or cattle, will be executed. I shall spare neither women nor children. I shall give the order to drive them away and fire on them. Such are my words to the Herero people. the Great General of the Mighty Kaiser, von Trotha.*" Some people spoke out in opposition to this mass extermination for economic reasons, since the colony needed workforce. But Trotha remained adamant, and as a result, 30,000 Herero died in the desert.

At the beginning of 1905, under international pressure and in response to interventions from members of the Social Democrat Party in the Reichstag, the extermination order was lifted, but not without difficulty. Extermination was followed by *Konzentrationslagern* (forced-labor camps). General von Bülow had the surviving Herero captured and parked in these camps, while the last of the land they had occupied was confiscated and divided among the settlers. The Herero initially worked for the military but were then made available to companies and later to civilians, often on a day-to-day basis.

Branded like cattle, classified as *arbeitsfähig* (fit) or *unfähig* (unfit), and forced to work like draft animals, they contributed to the construction of the railroad. The Herero suffered starvation, mistreatment, disease, exhaustion, rape, and murder and died in staggering numbers. Just three years after Trotha and his troops arrived in the region, there were only 15,000 Herero left. Although the camps were eventually dismantled in January 1908, following pressure from Social Democrats and human rights activists, the Herero did not regain their freedom. Each individual bore a number, and they were dispersed to farms to continue serving as laborers for the colonists. The Herero were exploited until the day they died.

Departments of anthropology and medicine at prestigious universities (Breslau and Berlin) received corpses and skulls, both as souvenirs brought back by soldiers returning from South-West Africa and in response to requests, to enable scientists to carry out experiments and prove the superiority of Europeans over Africans. The height of horror (although it is hard to say what the height was, given the number of atrocities that were committed) was the severed heads of children that adorned collectors' display cabinets.

THE ALAKALUF

....

Remembering the people

....

In 1520, when Magellan reached the southernmost tip of the American continent, he entered a strait to which he gave the name "Estrecho de todos los Santos," the Strait of All Saints. Large fires could be seen on land, revealing a human presence, and so, what had appeared to be a large island was christened Terra del Fuoco.

The Alakaluf were sea nomads who inhabited the archipelagos over a vast territory that stretched from Chiloé Island in the north to Cape Horn at the southern tip.

A few years later, Spanish navigator Garcia Jofré made a stopover here and met some "Indians." He was undoubtedly the first to make contact with the Kawésqar, as these sea nomads called themselves—meaning "men of skin and bones"—and later also known as the Alakaluf (which was how other tribes called them). These sea nomads inhabited the archipelagos over a vast territory stretching from Chiloé Island in the north to Cape Horn at the southern tip. In the southern part of western Patagonia, these populations were partially protected from the harsh weather by the relief. After passing the strait—a desolate place that appeared

to be populated by wretched, destitute people— the ships of the trading expeditions sailed for Peru. Starting in 1535, the Spaniards set out to conquer Chile. In turn, Diego de Almagro, Francisco de Ulloa, and, above all, Juan Ladrillero explored the extraordinary network of maritime channels. The writer of the expedition, Miguel de Goicueta, was the first to describe the natives, portraying them as poor folk. In the 1580s, Pedro Gómez Sarmiento completed his exploration of this labyrinth of sea arms, and he too described the locals as wretched and distrustful, but peaceful. This impression of good-naturedness was abruptly reversed with the massacre of Van Noort's expedition in 1598. For years afterward the Alakaluf were depicted in more-ferocious and inhumane terms. In 1624, Dutch navigator Jacob L'Hermite wrote, *"These savages are closer to beasts than to men; besides the fact that they tear men apart and devour their flesh raw and bloody, there is not the slightest trace of religion or order in them."* Throughout the seventeenth century, the methodical search for the fabulous City of the Caesars led to the exploration of the region by numerous missions flying various flags. In the 1740s, following a shipwreck, John Byron spent several months with the Alakaluf, learning to survive alongside them. In the eighteenth century, many of the Alakaluf's weaker, more structurally fragile neighbors, such as the Yahgan and Chono, disappeared, as did other peoples whose names have been forgotten. The Alakaluf and the Selk'nam

were perfectly adapted to the extreme conditions of their environment and remained for a long time the custodians of a frugal but original way of life that brought together a variety of cultures, a nomadic lifestyle, and reliance on the seasons and the environment. They survived by hunting sea lions and collecting shellfish.

At the end of the nineteenth century, the religious missions that settled in Tierra del Fuego stigmatized the natives' nudity and condemned their superstitions, severely undermining their way of life. At the same time, the British upset the millennia-old equilibrium the Alakaluf had survived on

The Alakaluf and the Selk'nam were perfectly adapted to the extreme conditions of their environment and remained for a long time the custodians of a frugal but original way of life that brought together a variety of cultures, a nomadic lifestyle, and reliance on the seasons and the environment.

by slaughtering colonies of sea lions that thrived in the region to use their blubber as oil to light up the streets of London. With their environment transformed and their numbers decimated by the diseases introduced by Europeans, the Alakaluf were about to embark on the irreversible journey that would lead to their extinction.

By 1900, their numbers had dwindled to just a thousand. Forty-six years later, when ethnologist José Emperaire arrived and recorded their history and customs in *Les Nomades de la mer* ("Nomads of the sea") before they disappeared forever, there were around a hundred. When he died tragically in 1958, there were only half that number left. In 1951, while exploring Patagonia, French writer and explorer Jean Raspail encountered strange people from another world. *"On the thirty-first day of our voyage, on the way back from a narrow pass between two islands that had captured the captain's full attention, we nearly split their motionless canoe in two. They were waiting for us. They were Alakaluf. I had imagined them. Now I saw them. Maybe I shouldn't have tempted reality. I won't forget them. Just as they are. I noted the position on the map. Longitude: W 74 degrees 12', latitude: S 53 degrees 37'. There were six of them in the boat. Three men, two women, and a child of about eight years old. They hadn't come from Puerto Eden, but 'from there,' they pointed towards a maze of dark channels that opens up at Cape Tama. And where were they going? 'Over there.' 'Over there' was Santa Inés Island, an unexplored mountain range covered with glaciers, battered by the Pacific and its huge waves, south of the Strait of Magellan. It was utterly inconceivable that any human life could cling to the island, and yet they were definitely pointing to that black-and-white mass over there."*

With their environment transformed and their numbers decimated by the diseases introduced by Europeans, the Alakaluf were about to embark on the vertiginous process that would lead to their extinction.

For years the writer was haunted by the vision of these poor souls. He mentioned them in several of his books and even dedicated a magnificent book to them: *Who Will Remember the People?* is a sobering foreshadowing of the extinction of the Alakaluf. Jean Raspail was right. Inbreeding, high infant mortality, and sterility wreaked irreversible havoc among the population. By the beginning of the twenty-first century, the Alakaluf had dwindled to just a dozen or so individuals scattered between Puerto Natales and Punta Arenas.

THE IK PEOPLE

From deconstruction to decline

The Ik people were long protected from contact with Europeans. They lived in the northern part of Uganda, northeast of Mount Morungole, the home of their god. For hundreds of years they were seminomadic, living in villages with circular huts protected by high palisades, each with its own granary.

In 1962, their lives were abruptly transformed by the government's decision to relocate them from their native region to reserves in the heart of a gigantic natural park. With the creation of this park, the Ik people had to put an end to their hunting activities and become breeders and farmers. This brutal change, decided upon at the highest level, had devastating repercussions on an unimaginable scale. It overturned their economic organization, their religious institutions, and their social and symbolic structures. The disintegration of Ik society was precipitated by the drought that hit the region and the terrible, long-lasting famine that followed in 1967. The society's unity was based on

The most recent and striking case of a society collapsing dramatically.

sharing wealth, and in particular the most important commodity: food. The introduction of agriculture had a considerable impact on the Ik people, who turned their backs on these values of altruism and solidarity and resorted to cattle raiding, bartering, and illegal hunting to earn a living.

The Ugandan government did not abandon the Ik people to their own demise and provided them with relief and assistance. But it did contribute to turning them into welfare recipients seeking to profit from the state. American anthropologist Colin Turnbull made several visits to the Ik people, notably when they faced drought and famine. In *The Mountain People*, published in 1972, he argues that human values can be annihilated only when survival is at stake. He described the Ik people as beings who had lost all humanity. While Colin Turnbull rightly alerted international opinion to an ethnocide whose speed was matched only by its spectacular nature, his book divided the scientific community.

In the 1980s, a cholera epidemic killed several hundred people in a population that had already dwindled to a few thousand. The Ik people have not disappeared, but they represent the most recent and striking case of a society collapsing dramatically.

PEOPLES STILL UNDER THREAT

My people are few. They resemble the scattering trees of a storm-swept plain. . . . There was a time when our people covered the land as the waves of a wind-ruffled sea cover its shell-paved floor, but that time long since passed away with the greatness of tribes that are now but a mournful memory.

—*Chief Seattle of the Duwamish Native American tribe to Governor Isaac Stevens, following the signing of the Point Elliott Treaty in 1855*

Not far from Mount Williams, in Launceston, northeastern Tasmania, is the starting point of the wukalina walk, a walking tour linking the bush to the beaches of the Bay of Fires. Tourists walk it alongside local people speaking palawa kani, a language made up of the nine languages once spoken on the island, which have been eradicated along with the last remaining speakers. The walk is a memorial trail to make sure the Tasmanian Aboriginal people are never forgotten. On Namibia's Shark Island, opposite a monument to the German soldiers who fell in 1905, the descendants of Captain Joseph Fredericks, a resistance leader, erected a stele in his memory. The Herero and Nama peoples are constantly working to ensure that the memory of the unfinished extermination that decimated their ancestors a century ago is not forgotten. Skulls and bones that had been sent to university laboratories during Germany's Second Reich were returned to a Herero delegation to be buried in Namibia, in the land of their ancestors. In 2007, the descendants of General von Trotha apologized to the descendants of the Herero and Nama

victims of their forefathers' crimes. This symbolic but powerful gesture was necessary for dialogue, and even reconciliation, to take place.

"Who are the Aztecs of our time?" asked playwright Michel Azama, as he evoked the millions of deaths that resulted from the "discovery" of America, the fifth centenary of which was celebrated in 1992. Who are these civilizations? Who are these peoples? Who are these ethnic groups facing a bleak future?

As this journey across the globe and through time comes to its end, a conclusion can be reached: the reality and facts are terrible, sometimes apocalyptic, but sadly unforgiving. Extinction has affected both peoples numbering a hundred or so individuals with a rudimentary way of life, such as the Pitcairn Islanders, or the inhabitants of Henderson and Mangareva Islands, as well as hierarchical civilizations governed by a king or emperor, with castes of priests, elders, soldiers, and craftsmen, such as the Egyptians, the Incas, and the Songhai. As they disappeared, the customs, techniques, legislation, arts, and religious beliefs, sometimes down to the last representatives of these civiliza-

tions, as was the case with the Aboriginal Tasmanians, also vanished. Gone are the happy Harappans of the Indus valley, gone are the refined
Etruscans, gone are the ingenious Phoenicians,
the brilliant Moche, the celestial Anasazi . . . they
have all vanished. And if it was not populations
and individuals that became extinct, it was their
way of life that faded away. What remains today of
the traditions of the Gulyak that Anton Chekhov
met when he visited Sakhalin Island? What is left
of the cosmological knowledge and mythological beliefs of the Inuit, whose existence was first
recorded by French explorer and anthropologist
Jean Malaurie in the 1950s?

The causes behind the disappearance of these
peoples and civilizations were always the same:
a climatic catastrophe, such as the droughts that
struck the Mayan civilization and precipitated
the end of the Tang dynasty, the severe and er-
ratic monsoons that shook the Khmer Empire, or
large-scale deforestation and destruction of resources or the environment, as was the case with
the Maya; hostile enemies in the case of the Native
Americans, the Tasmanians, and the Herero and
Nama; or the disappearance of trading partners,
such as in the case of the Pitcairn Islanders. Any
one of these causes alone could have been enough
to plunge a people or a civilization into chaos.

But oftentimes, several of these factors came together. That said, the ultimate element that sealed
all their destinies was the reactions and the way
these peoples and civilizations chose to respond
to the crises they faced. Many peoples and civilizations made unfortunate choices that contributed, as much as the principal causes, to their disintegration, collapse, or destruction.

While climatic catastrophes are difficult to pre-
dict, and while we hope to believe that genocides
and ethnocides belong to the past (such as the Ar-
menian genocide, which the Turkish government
has still not recognized, or the genocides in former Yugoslavia and Rwanda), natural resources
are not infinite. In too many parts of the planet,
massive deforestation, the thoughtless dumping
of toxic waste and sewage, groundwater pollution,
and the consequences of equally ill-considered
actions threaten people in the Amazon, Africa,
the Far North, and Oceania a little more every day.
On countless Pacific islands, sacred lands are still
being violated; traditions, customs, and cultures
are being trampled; and languages are being threatened. In Asia, the Hmong people have been the victims of violence and discrimination for decades. The
situation of the Batwa, who are still facing difficul-
ties relating to land rights, remains worrying, and in
China, the Uyghurs living in the Xinjiang Uyghur
Autonomous Region in the west of the country still
face extraordinarily violent repression.

Minorities and Indigenous peoples are not the
only ones threatened with disintegration. In his

Who are these civilizations?
Who are these peoples? Who
are these ethnic groups facing a
bleak future?

masterful book *Collapse: How Societies Choose to Fail or Succeed*, Jared Diamond shows, with figures, decrees, and laws, how in the space of less than a century, a state with an abundance of minerals, excellent timber, and diverse fauna has—as a result of choices made by managers of small operations and large companies, the inhabitants, and the governments in charge—wrecked its environment to such an extent that current generations are suffering and future generations will pay a heavy price. This state is not in Africa, Asia, or the Pacific. It is one of America's largest states, long dubbed "Big Sky Country": Montana. His unforgiving, unapologetic, and alarming report is a stark but sobering reminder that all civilizations are mortal.

ACKNOWLEDGMENTS

At the end of these wanderings among the world's civilizations and peoples, I would like to extend my warmest thanks to my editors, Valérie Dumeige and Karine Do Vale, for giving me the opportunity to embark on this painful but necessary journey through time and space, and for their collaboration, which has always been as fruitful as it has been invaluable. I would also like to thank Camille Renversade for his wonderful and bewitching illustrations, and Vivien Boyer for his unconditional support. Finally, I would like to thank my wife, Stefanie, and my daughter, Justine. Thanks to all six of you! Without you this book simply would not have been possible. Camille Renversade would also like to thank Sonia Delbost-Henry, Amandine Puntous, Pascal Labbe, Alma Forrer, Cécile and Gilles Patissier, and Bernadette Gouvernayre.

BOOKS IN THE SAME SERIES

Atlas of Dream Lands, Dominique Lanni, illustrations by Karin Doering-Froger, 2023

Atlas of Elementary Botany, Jean-Jacques Rousseau, 2025

Atlas of Extraterrestrial Zones, Bruno Fuligni, illustrations by François Moreno, 2023

Atlas of Lost Paradises, Gilles Lapouge, illustrations by Karin Doering-Froger, 2024

Atlas of Shipwrecks and Fortunes of the Sea, Cyril Hofstein, illustrations by Karin Doering-Froger, 2024

Dominique Lanni is a professor at the University of Malta and specializes in the modes of representation of otherness and travel literature. He has published *Bestiaire fantastique des voyageurs* (2014), *Atlas of Dream Lands* (2015), *Heureux qui, comme Hannibal* (2020), and *Mary* (2022).

Camille Renversade is an artist, author-illustrator, and sculptor who graduated from the École Émile-Cohl in Lyon. He specializes in cryptozoology and has produced seven books on the subject, including *Créatures Fantastiques Deyrolle*, published by Plume de carotte, as well as numerous artistic creations.